To Win Just Once

The Life of the Journeyman Jump Jockey

Sean Magee and Guy Lewis

HEADLINE

First published in 1997
by HEADLINE BOOK PUBLISHING

First published in paperback in 1998
by HEADLINE BOOK PUBLISHING

10 9 8 7 6 5 4 3 2 1

ISBN 0 7472 5818 X

Set in 11/15 Sabon by Production Line, Oxford
Printed and bound in Great Britain by
Mackays of Chatham PLC, Chatham, Kent

HEADLINE BOOK PUBLISHING
A division of Hodder Headline PLC
338 Euston Road
London NW1 3BH

Contents

In memory of
RICHARD DAVIS
1969–1996

Preface

The Ten O'Clock News

O N THE EVENING OF FRIDAY 19 JULY 1996 I TURNED on the radio to catch the ten o'clock news while cooking supper.

The bulletin chronicled the horrific rape and murder of an English schoolgirl in France; government reaction to a postal workers' dispute; the search off Long Island for the flight recorders following the crash of TWA flight 800; the attempt to bring Radovan Karadzic before a war crimes tribunal; the RUC chief constable's resistance to calls for his resignation; the clearance for families of children who had contracted CJD to seek compensation; Cambridge University's acceptance of a hefty donation from one of the world's largest manufacturers of cigarettes; the Ministry of Defence's announcement that the Duke of York was to leave the Royal Navy in three years' time. Then came this:

> The National Hunt jockey Richard Davis has died in hospital after a fall during a race at

Southwell this afternoon. His mount fell at the first fence during a novices' handicap chase, and crushed him.

The centennial Olympic Games gets under way in the American city of Atlanta in just under four hours' time. Eighty-five thousand people, including the Princess Royal, will attend the extravagant opening ceremony . . .

Four days earlier, on the Monday of that week, I had had lunch with Richard Davis at The Plough in Ford, the great Cotswold racing pub, liberally decorated with photos of famous horses and races, hard by the foot of David Nicholson's gallops not far from Stow-on-the-Wold. We had been discussing a book project we were cooking up: to work together through the coming season to describe the ups and downs, the exhilarations and depressions, of the life of the 'ordinary' jump jockey.

We would build on the foundations laid in the diary Richard had been keeping during the previous season in collaboration with his neighbour Keith Knight, and describe the world of the rider who is not Richard Dunwoody or Tony McCoy but without whose participation the sport would not continue, the rider who lives in constant hope of that one big opportunity, perhaps a chance ride on a good horse, which will pluck him out of the ranks and place him firmly on the upward escalator.

Richard was in high spirits that Monday at The Plough (though not so high that he would forget that as a jockey he had always to watch his weight: jacket potato for lunch, but hold the butter). He had recently returned from his first riding visit to the Czech Republic, and his story of that trip epitomised both his sense of fun and the core of professionalism that underlay it. He had brought with him a map of the extraordinarily convoluted Pardubice cross-country course – while out there he had studied the plan and walked the course for hours, only to discover shortly before his race that his horse had been withdrawn – and talked me through this with all the enthusiasm of the motorist showing you a new route to Uttoxeter. He also regaled me with tales of late-night shenanigans in the hotel night club which, the visiting British jockeys discovered, doubled as the local brothel. By way of contrast, just before that Czech trip he had been to Royal Ascot, and proudly brought out photographs of himself resplendent in morning suit.

We parted in the pub car park, Richard letting his dog Henry – an ebullient Jack Russell – out of his car for a quick scamper on the grass. Let's speak again soon, I suggested as he pursued Henry: what are you doing later this week? I'm schooling a horse for a trainer on Wednesday, he said; riding at Southwell on Friday, going to a wedding on Saturday; I'll phone you Sunday.

That Friday morning a vet friend called in, and as we sat in the kitchen drinking coffee, we skimmed through the pages of the racing press. I noticed that Richard was going to Southwell for just one ride, on a nag called Mr Sox, a horse with no chance whatsoever. This was the very crux of what we had been talking about in The Plough a few days earlier – the necessity for the journeyman jump jockey to flog halfway across the country to ride a useless horse with no possibility of winning. Why was he doing it? I'll ring Richard, I told my friend, and ask him to jot down a few thoughts about this, which we could then use in the book.

But I never made that call, and a few hours later on that steaming hot July evening two brief sentences on Radio Four delivered the numbing news that I never would.

Guy Lewis will not mind my saying this, but this book should have been written with Richard.

When that option became impossible, my first reaction was to ditch the whole idea. But what had happened to Richard was so central to the position of the journeyman jockey in National Hunt racing that I began to think that a book describing that life might, in some way, serve as a form of memorial to him.

Having decided to persevere I was blessed in finding Guy Lewis as a guide through the jump jockey's world. The connection was appropriate. Guy's sister Zoë had been Richard's girlfriend; Guy and Richard had been close friends; Guy had been on the recent trip to the Czech Republic; like Richard (though still a conditional jockey), Guy was struggling to find the path which leads upwards from early promise towards a place in the sun; and, also like Richard, Guy was not shy of delivering his opinions.

As it turned out, the 1996–7 season was not an easy one for Guy, and did not deliver the results he (and I) had been hoping for when we got together on this book. But his optimism at even the most depressing times, his patience as I asked stupid questions and his candour in detailing his own feelings at (occasional) moments of great frustration have been invaluable, and I am grateful to him for his cheerful participation. I am also grateful to him for his ability to hide his disappointment when he realised that the call on the mobile phone was not some trainer offering a ride, but (yet again) me with that most awkward of questions: where are you riding next week? Today's jockey cannot exist without his mobile, and although it was quite usual to have my call answered in some racecourse sauna or in the car nudging double the speed limit on the M5, it was none the less a surprise to realise, when phoning Guy early one morning in the spring, that he was taking the call on horseback while riding out in Lambourn . . .

This book would not exist at all without Guy, but many others have helped in its construction. Richard's parents Ann and John Davis, and his brothers Andrew and Stephen, have been immensely helpful and hospitable, as have Guy's parents Roger and June Lewis and his sisters Zoë and Hannah. Jo Davies provided me with all sorts of intimate details about Guy, most of which I am far too discreet to repeat.

Thanks are due to The Saw Doctors for permission to quote the words of 'To Win Just Once', and to use that song's title as the title of this book.

Particular thanks to Katrina Whone, lay reader; to Phillip Jones, indefatigable researcher; to David Pipe and John Maxse of the Jockey Club; to Robert Cooper of The Racing Channel; to Lucy Ash; to Brian Brivati; to Lisa Rogers; to Lucy Tallon; to Andrew Parker; and to all in racing who have furnished details, explanations, and opinions.

At Headline, I am grateful to Alan Brooke for his enthusiasm for the idea before he was unseated (or should that read 'brought down'?); to Celia Kent, implacable as ever; to Heather Holden-Brown; and most of all to Lorraine Jerram: her plaintive weekly enquiry, 'Have you written *any* of this book?', will live with me for ever – or at least until the next book is due.

And yet again the Rapid Reaction Force of Charlie Webster (keyboards) and Gillian Bromley (synthesiser) made possible what otherwise would have been impossible.

S.M.
July 1997

List of Illustrations

1

A Country Funeral

'An honest heart and an open mind'

RICHARD DAVIS'S FUNERAL TOOK PLACE IN THE thirteenth-century village church of St Nicholas in Earls Croome, Worcestershire, one warm, sunny Friday in late July 1996. His death just one week earlier at the age of twenty-six, following a fall in a steeplechase at Southwell, had stunned the world of National Hunt racing, and now the famous and the lowly from that world gathered at the tiny church to mourn one of their number killed in action.

Long before the start of the funeral at noon the interior of the church was full, with recordings of Don McLean and the Irish band The Saw Doctors playing softly to remind the congregation of Richard Davis's favourite music. On the grassy banks flanking the path to the church door stood a throng of mourners – some talking quietly, most silently contemplating the photograph of the young man whose characteristically grinning features under a mud-spattered crash helmet looked out from the front of the order of service.

Among the mourners were many jockeys who had shared the glories and dangers of riding over jumps, there to express the collective grief of the weighing room: leading riders such as Richard Dunwoody, Adrian Maguire, Jamie Osborne and the freshly crowned champion Tony McCoy, as well as those whose presence recalled the darker side of the sport, such as Richard's great friend Dai Tegg, whose riding career was curtailed by a brain haemorrhage following a succession of falls.

All had come to honour a life as well as mourn a death, and celebration of that life pervaded the funeral service. After the sentences were pronounced as the coffin was borne up the aisle of the church to rest in front of the altar, the congregation sang out the most life-affirming of hymns, 'All Things Bright and Beautiful'.

Then Richard Dunwoody, three times champion and the finest rider of his generation, moved to the lectern to deliver the words of the Saw Doctors song that had become an anthem for the jump jockeys:

> To win just once would be enough
> For those who've lost in life or love
> For those who've lost their guile and nerve
> Their innocence, their drive and verve
> For those who feel they've been mistreated
> Discriminated, robbed or cheated
> To claim one victory inspired
> To win just once is their desire
>
> To win just once
> To win just once

To win just once
That would be enough

To win just once against the odds
And once be smiled on by the gods
To race with speed along the track
Break the tape and not look back
To never have considered losing
As if to win is by your choosing
Bare your soul for all to find
An honest heart and an open mind

To win just once
To win just once
To win just once
That would be enough

So come all ye full-time small-town heroes
Cast away your inbred fears of
Standing out from all the rest
The cynics and the pessimists
The self-indulgent, almost rich
The blatant hurlers on the ditch
Time is passing so come on
And face the ball, the game is on

To win just once
To win just once
To win just once
That would be enough.

And so the service proceeded, personal and professional elements intertwining: an address from Michael Caulfield, Secretary of the Jockeys' Association; a recording of Don McLean singing 'American Pie', Richard's favourite song; prayers; a final hymn, 'Fight the Good Fight' ('Run the straight race through God's good grace . . . '); the commendation and the blessing. Then, as the coffin was taken back down the aisle, a representative of the Worcestershire Hunt sounded a haunting call on the horn: Gone Away.

The coffin was borne to the far end of St Nicholas' churchyard where, in the presence of his immediate family, Richard Davis's body was lowered into the ground. The family returned to rejoin the rest of the congregation, and for the next half hour a long stream of mourners wound its way slowly past the grave. Each paused briefly to pay his or her own respects to the man described in the following day's racing press as 'jump racing's fallen warrior'. Some sent a handful of earth clattering on to the coffin lid below.

On the headstone which now marks the grave, the letters 'RIP' are enclosed in a horseshoe.

What had happened to Richard Davis was this.

He was riding a horse named Mr Sox in the Fisherton Novices' Handicap Chase at Southwell, Nottinghamshire, on 19 July 1996. Mr Sox, his only ride of the day and a horse he had never ridden in a race before, was one of hundreds of animals who occupy the deepest basement of the racehorse world. Now aged five and a gelding, he had been switched to jumping after a completely undistinguished career on the Flat – no form from five outings as a two- and three-year-old. In his first hurdle race at Ludlow he started at 100–1 and was tailed off behind the rest of the field when pulled up. He was then sent steeplechasing. Starting at 100–1 in a novices' chase, again at Ludlow, he blundered at the first fence and unseated his rider at the sixth. Back over hurdles at Stratford, yet again 100–1, he managed to complete the course, finishing a remote eighth; in his fourth race over jumps he was tailed off and pulled up in a hurdle race at Southwell. The Jockey Club inquiry into Richard Davis's death would state that Mr Sox's official rating of 60 put him in the bottom 2.86 per cent of the 1,500 or so racehorses with ratings over fences; only thirteen horses in training were on a lower mark. In the prim terminology of the racing form book, Mr Sox was 'of no account'. In the more robust parlance of punters, he was useless.

In the Fisherton Novices' Handicap Chase at Southwell he started rank outsider in a field of six runners. Having made the short run from the start to the first fence, Mr Sox failed to judge his take-off correctly. Although he just managed to get his front legs over the fence, his hind quarters did not give him enough power to clear it properly, and his underside slammed into the birch. The impact of hitting the fence so comprehensively at a speed of around thirty miles an hour flipped the horse's rear end into the air and his head sharply downwards, and as he descended steeply Richard Davis was shot over his head. Half a second after the jockey hit the ground the full three-quarters of a ton of Mr Sox, pivoting on his nose, somersaulted down squarely on top of him. Mr Sox quickly regained his feet and made off after the other runners.

Richard Davis, in the gruesome jargon of jump jockeys 'buried' by his horse, was knocked out by the impact of the fall and lay on the ground as the paramedics who had been tracking the runners in an ambulance (as, according to Jockey Club regulations, they must) rushed to attend him. At the subsequent inquest the first paramedic on the scene described how the jockey was lying on his side, unconscious, blue in the face and showing signs of respiratory distress: 'I went to the patient's head to keep his head still because in cases like this there is the risk of head injury. Every time he breathed there was a noise. I shouted at the patient to see if he could hear me. There was no response even though his eyes were open. I waved my hand in front of his eyes; again there was no response. His skin colour turned from blue to pale and he was very sweaty.'

As Davis was gingerly placed on to a spine board in order that he could be stretchered off the course, he began to regain consciousness and respond to the paramedics' questions: 'He was unaware of the day and the date and the Prime Minister's name and the horse's details, etc. He kept repeating, "I came on my own and I have already had my spleen removed."'

Davis was taken to the racecourse medical centre, where he had to wait ten minutes for a county ambulance to arrive and take him to hospital. (The paramedic ambulance could not itself take him as another Jockey Club regulation states that there must be two ambulances in attendance when a race is run: had one of these been otherwise engaged in taking the stricken jockey off for proper treatment, the sport would have been held up.) During the wait Davis was conscious enough to ask for painkillers for his back, and to fret about what would happen to his beloved dog, Henry. His racecourse valet Tom Buckingham gathered his clothes, wallet and other effects and took them out to the ambulance. Fellow jockey Warren Marston made arrangements about his car: after racing he would drive it from the course to a trainer's yard from where Richard could collect it. These practical procedures are routine. Jump jockeys don't always get home that night.

As the runners for the second race that afternoon made their way on to the racecourse from the parade ring, the jockeys glanced anxiously across at their comrade being loaded on a stretcher into the county ambulance – which the racecourse doctor, under the impression that Richard had incurred back injuries, instructed to drive slowly to the nearest large hospital, the Queen's Medical Centre in Nottingham, some dozen miles from the course.

At the hospital Richard Davis underwent surgery, and only now did the extent of the damage to his crushed internal organs become apparent. His inferior vena cava – the main vein of the body which leads into the heart – had been torn three-quarters of the way across, flooding his abdomen with between four and five pints of blood, and his liver had been split. (Remarkably, not a single bone in his body had been broken.) During surgery the severe haemorrhaging and shock due to loss of blood caused his heart to arrest. He was pronounced dead at 5.40 p.m., three hours and twenty minutes after Mr Sox had tried to jump that first fence.

The official cause of death was given as a lacerated liver combined with severe, uncontrollable internal bleeding.

His estate would receive his fee for riding Mr Sox: £80.

*

Richard Davis's death sent shock waves reverberating through the world of racing. On the Saturday, the day after the accident, racegoers at the day's six meetings stood for a minute's silence. In the sweltering heat of the Stratford meeting on the Sunday, Richard Dunwoody led his fellow jockeys in an act of remembrance, placing flowers under the number 1 marker board in the unsaddling enclosure. The racecard that day had R. Davis down to ride a horse named Magic Bloom in the 3.40: jockeys for that race had been officially declared on the previous Friday morning, as Richard Davis was driving to Southwell.

As the immediate shock gave way to reflection, questions began to be asked. Was Mr Sox just too wretched a horse to be racing at all? Had he been running that day with a fractured pelvis? Was his trainer Laura Shally – who had nine horses in her yard under a 'permit', which allowed her to train only for members of her own family and not for any other owner – qualified to be training? Was Southwell racecourse, and in particular the area around that fatal first fence, safe? Were the medical facilities at the track satisfactory – why had the racecourse doctor not suspected the full extent of the jockey's injuries, and had there been unnecessary delay in bringing him proper medical attention at hospital?

Worm after worm wriggled out of the can, some with literally poisonous intent. A fortnight after the accident, three horses in Laura Shally's yard died. Had they been poisoned in a perverse attempt to seek revenge for the jockey's death?

While the shades of Dick Francis deepened, above the rumbling controversies the fate that befell Richard Davis focused attention more closely than ever on the professional jump jockeys, on that small of group of individuals for whom the disproportion between risk and reward is so great as to mark them off from other professional sportsmen as a band apart.

In particular, it focused attention on the ordinary grafters of the weighing room, the 'journeymen' jockeys (to borrow the American term rapidly gaining currency in Britain) who form the backbone of the sport. They risk life and limb for a financial return risible by the standards of many other sports. Why?

What happened to Richard Davis could have happened to Richard Dunwoody or Tony McCoy, but the fact that his fall was from such an inadequate animal as Mr Sox pinpointed the eternal dilemma of the struggling jump jockey: whether to accept rides on horses which you know to be unreliable, dangerous, or simply bad. Generally the question is academic, because you are in no position to be picky. You need every ride you can get in order to keep on making your presence – however obscure – felt, in order to keep your face and your name in the minds of owners and trainers and your place in the fabric of the sport, in order to be there to pick up the spare ride one afternoon which might just lift you another rung up the ladder. Maybe that bad horse will run away with you; maybe it will bury you; maybe it will kill you. But say 'no thanks' too often and you're on a downward slope steeper than the back straight at Plumpton.

The journeyman can graduate towards the upper echelons of his profession only by keeping in the thick of the action. And that means keeping himself in the firing line.

The sight of the ambulance tracking the runners in each race is a sobering reminder of the risks involved, and so are the statistics. A jump jockey can expect to have a fall once every fourteen rides, and the incident which cost Richard Davis his life is repeated almost daily on the racecourses of Great Britain and Ireland. The history of the sport is peppered with riders, both the great and the ordinary, whose careers have been brought to an untimely end by injury. (There are also plenty of notable careers for whom a fall has simply been one tumble too far. John Francome, for many observers the finest jump jockey of the modern era, decided that enough was enough at Chepstow in 1985: 'I parted company with The Reject at the open ditch in the straight and as he did so he galloped all over me. I am not superstitious as a rule but I took this as a hint that it was time to pack up and so that's what I did.')

In 1996 Dr Michael Turner, medical consultant to the Jockey Club, undertook an analysis of the danger of racing – Flat and National Hunt – compared with other sports. While evidence in such an area is notoriously ambiguous, not to say unreliable (the very notion of 'injury', for example, covers a wide variety of conditions), Dr Turner concluded that in terms of the rate of fatalities, jump racing is four times as dangerous as motor racing, and less dangerous only than climbing, air sports and (significantly) riding in point-to-points. Richard Davis was the sixth jockey to be killed in action in Britain since Joe Blanks died of head injuries following a fall in a Flat race at Brighton in July 1981. Of the other five, four – Michael Blackmore, Jayne Thompson, Vivian Kennedy and Philip Barnard – died following injuries in hurdle races, and the sixth – Steve Wood – in a Flat race.

The danger is well known and well appreciated, but efforts to minimise the risk, for example by wearing protective clothing, can go only so far towards preventing serious injury. Today's jockeys must wear officially approved crash helmets and body protectors, but, according to Michael Turner, 'in Richard's case there was nothing that could have prevented the injuries other than not riding.'

National Hunt racing is a visceral sport: its cocktail of strength, speed, noise, colour, muscle, leather unlocks deep emotions. And for those of us who stand at the wings of the fences and feel our waters tingling as that thunder in the depths of the earth rolls ever louder, then *ooohhh!* and *aaahhh!* as the runners flash into view and launch themselves over the fence, land in a swirl of legs and flying birch and gallop off, the thunder subsiding, it is easy to get carried away, to rhapsodise about the bravery of jump jockeys, to become dewy-eyed quoting the Will H. Ogilvie poem about the riders

> Taking what the Fates provide them,
> Danger calling, Death beside them. –
> 'Tis a game beyond gainsaying
> Made by gods for brave men's playing.

Day to day, the jump jockey's life is rather less romantic, and the fallout from Richard Davis's death – statements about the torn inferior vena cava, the wrangling over ambulance arrangements, the hounding of the unfortunate trainer – brought home the stark reality of the risks. It was the appreciation of that reality, the acknowledgement that 'there but for the grace of God', that bonded together all those from the world of jump racing who had gathered at St Nicholas' church that sunny July afternoon. Not one of the jockeys among the mourners was blind to the fact that what had happened to Richard at Southwell could so easily have happened to him – least of all, perhaps, Richard's close friend and brother of his girlfriend Zoë, Guy Lewis, a young rider himself struggling to make the grade after a career of great early promise had gone cold.

Not that Guy could afford to dwell on this. After the funeral a group of the jockeys repaired to The Plough at Ford, one of the great racing pubs of the Cotswolds, for an informal wake which would go on long into the night. But Guy Lewis decided to go home and spend a quiet evening. He was riding at Stratford the following day.

2

Guy

*'None of them ever impressed me
as much as Guy Lewis'*

EARLY ON THE MORNING AFTER RICHARD'S funeral Guy Lewis left home – his parents' farm at Llanmartin, near Chepstow just over the Welsh border from the Severn Bridge – and drove the hour and a half to Stratford racecourse for his thirteenth ride of the season which had begun in June 1996 and would finish at the end of May 1997.

On arrival in the weighing room he presented his medical book to show that he was officially declared fit to ride, then located his peg in the changing room: the blue and white colours of his one ride that afternoon, Channel Pastime, were already hanging there. He changed into his riding gear; weighed himself on the 'trying scales' to check that he was the correct weight for his ride; was officially weighed out by the Clerk of the Scales; handed his saddle over to Channel Pastime's trainer Dai Burchell; and returned to the changing room to await the call for the jockeys to file out to the parade ring.

Channel Pastime – a twelve-year-old gelding a little past his best but an old favourite of his jockey's and a much more reliable conveyance than many of the horses Guy was used to riding – ran his usual honest race in the three-mile steeple-chase, clearing the eighteen fences and running on at one pace to finish third. This performance earned his owner £524, and his jockey £23.12 – calculated as a percentage of the total prize money, as laid down in the Rules of Racing – in addition to his riding fee of £84.80.

Having dismounted in the unsaddling enclosure, taken the saddle off Channel Pastime and passed post-race comments to owner and trainer, Guy returned to the weighing room. He weighed in, changed out of his riding gear, showered and drove the hour and a half back to South Wales.

At the beginning of that season Guy Lewis was one of some 170 licensed professional jump jockeys. Of that number, about half were fully fledged riders; the others, including Guy, were 'conditional' jockeys, the jumping equivalent of apprentices, young riders aspiring to join the senior ranks. This small band of sportsmen – and a very few women – exert a peculiar hold on the imagination of the sporting public, a fascination out of all proportion to their public profile. Few are familiar figures outside their sport, but the very nature of what they do intrigues, enthrals – even humbles – observers.

So what *do* they do? They ride horses in hurdle races and steeplechases: steer them, galvanise them at each jump, put them right if they blunder, position them through the race to maximise their chances, urge and cajole them for their greatest effort at the climax of each contest.

In a hurdle race this involves galloping at about thirty miles an hour over obstacles like sheep hurdles, three foot six high – at least four of them every mile – for anything between two and three and a half miles. In steeplechases the obstacles are more solid – made of birch packed densely into a frame – and bigger: the minimum is four foot six inches high. Steeplechase fences confront horse and jockey more frequently than hurdles: there are at least six of them per mile, and they include variations such as the open ditch – a fence preceded by an exposed ditch, protected by a guard rail – and the water jump, a much lower fence followed by an expanse of water. (Increasingly unpopular with many followers of jump racing, water jumps are no longer a compulsory feature of a steeplechase, and have been removed from some courses.) The shortest steeplechase, over two miles, takes about four minutes; the longest, the Grand National over four and a half miles, about ten.

Although race riding forms the sharp end of the jockey's life, action on the racecourse is only part of his professional duties: an essential related activity is riding out for trainers, assessing and 'schooling' horses – teaching them to jump – and in the process impressing his own abilities on the mind of the trainers on whom his livelihood in large part depends.

In Flat racing the jockey's principal aim in a race is to harness and then deploy the speed which has been bred into his partner. For a jump jockey that is only part of the assignment. Equally crucial is guiding the horse at speed towards each obstacle so that it jumps fluently. Ask the experts what is the key characteristic of the best jump jockeys of the modern era – John Francome, Richard Dunwoody – and they will talk of the ability to 'present' a horse at a fence, that knack of measuring the rapidly diminishing distance between you and the next obstacle, adjusting your mount's action a few strides before he meets the jump so that he will sail over serenely and resume his gallop on the other side.

What is particularly piquant about the jump jockey's calling is the level of risk involved in relation to the level of reward on offer. Steering three-quarters of a ton of racehorse at thirty miles an hour twelve times or more over four foot six of birch clearly brings with it a high level of danger; yet very few jump jockeys make more than a very basic living, and the many for whom winners are few and far between have to struggle by on riding fees, with considerable expenses to be taken into account.

The leading practitioners of all major sports are fascinating, riveting purely because they are so good. With the majority of those sportsmen and sportswomen, spectators are captivated by their excellence, their ability to do something accessible at an infinitely higher level than you can. Watch Martina Hingis or Stephen Hendry or Shane Warne or Alan Shearer, and you may swoon at their sheer ability, but you know how it feels to play that game; it's just that they play it so much better.

But there are a few sports where the casual observer simply cannot imagine what it must be like to take part. What does it feel like to ski jump, to shoot down the slope, take off and soar high into the air with that extraordinary grace? What must it feel like to bobsleigh, to cram yourself into a canister and, without any serious mechanism for braking, hurtle at eighty miles an hour down a chute which may be built from ice but appears to have the consistency of concrete? Similarly, what can it possibly feel like to ride a top-class two-mile chaser down the back straight at Sandown Park, or a headstrong, unschooled novice hurdler in a field of twenty around Warwick, when you know that in that scrum your partner can no more get a proper view of each approaching hurdle than you can?

Many sports are dangerous, many athletes display a bravery to which the only possible response by the couch potatoes who watch them is to shake their heads in wonderment and open another lager. What makes the jump jockey's calling unusually hazardous is his partner in the athletic enterprise, the horse – a large and powerful creature whose muscles generate immensely more force than his own and are controlled by signals from that most inscrutable of equine organs, the size of a man's fist, which all who have ridden will recognise as being located halfway between themselves and the horizon, with an ear on each side: the horse's brain.

Research has described how during the Eocene epoch, some 55 million years ago, what set the horse apart from his fellow herbivores was a significantly larger brain, and in particular an expanded neocortex – the part of the brain responsible for learning. So the attraction of the horse as a working domestic animal was rooted in its combination of size, strength and biddability.

Biddability? Tell that to Walter Swinburn as he lies in intensive care in Hong Kong in February 1996 after a two-year-old he was riding had veered diagonally across the track after leaving the starting stalls, and then shot off in the opposite direction and crashed into the running rail. Tell it to

Peter Scudamore as he trudges back to the weighing room at Cheltenham in January 1989 after his mount Tarconey has, for no apparent reason at all, ducked out at full gallop and crashed into the wing of the final fence when the race was in his grasp. Tell it to Guy Lewis as he gives vent to his exasperation on Chan The Man, who is standing knee-deep in the River Severn hard by Worcester racecourse and resolutely refusing to budge in November 1995 after failing to negotiate the home turn in the bumper; or as Guy picks himself up from the ground in the parade ring at Bangor-on-Dee in December 1996 after Cashel Quay has reared up and fallen over backwards on him. Horses may be good learners, but no one can ever know exactly what is going on in that brain.

It is said that riders on the Flat are the better jockeys, in the narrow sense of getting the horse to run as fast as he possibly can, while their National Hunt counterparts are the better all-round horsemen, since their job involves the additional responsibility of controlling the horse's jumping – no easy matter when you are hurtling towards a steeplechase fence at speed. The nature of a horse's vision means that at the moment of taking off it cannot actually see the jump at all: it has to rely on the image of that jump imprinted a stride or two before take-off. Some horses seem to have such a very short memory span that they cannot remember even that far back, and those are the careless, often downright dangerous horses with whom it is the lot of the journeyman jockey to be associated.

There is a particular hazard associated with riding novices. A novices' hurdle or a novices' steeplechase is a race for horses which have not won a hurdle or chase respectively before 1 May the previous season. That is, they are inexperienced, and experience is a vital asset in a horse racing at speed over obstacles: the ability to adapt to the circumstances at a fence, to put in a short stride and 'fiddle' safely to the other side, can spell the difference between falling and staying in the race.

If it is the usual lot of the journeyman jockey to ride the worst horses, the down-and-outs of the equine race, it is also their lot to spend most of their time plying their trade not at the glamorous locations like Cheltenham, Sandown Park or Ascot but at the 'gaff' tracks, the small, mostly locally supported circuits which are the bread-and-butter arenas of the sport. Real jumping enthusiasts love the gaffs, would rather be at Kelso or Hexham or Towcester than Doncaster or Haydock Park, and would find having to make a decision between Cartmel on a Bank Holiday Monday and higher-class racing at some more swanky venue no contest. They love the gaffs, and they love the jockeys who provide those courses with their sport. Those privileged to have been present at both Frankie Dettori's seven-timer at Ascot in September 1996 and Richard Guest's four-timer at Cartmel in May 1997 would have found the former occasion a model of restraint in comparison with the mood of the latter.

The small jumping tracks have no pretensions. Nor do the riders whose names feature regularly on their number boards.

Wales has produced a series of great National Hunt jockeys – among them the Anthony brothers, Ivor, Jack and Owen; the Rees brothers, Fred and Lewis; and Fulke Walwyn. In recent years riders such as Carl Llewellyn, Neale Doughty and Hywel Davies have maintained the tradition.

Guy Lewis was born in Newport, Gwent, on 17 November 1974 into the sort of family from which so many of the great National Hunt jockeys have come, a dynasty of devotion to horses and jump racing bequeathed from generation to generation. (Richard Davis's father John had in the 1950s worked at Fairlawne for the great trainer Peter Cazalet, and had ridden gallops on such famous horses as Lochroe and Devon Loch.)

Guy's paternal grandfather Wilfred had ridden in point-to-points, and his father Roger Lewis did so for twenty-one seasons – from the age of fourteen until he was thirty-five – winning some thirty races 'between the flags' and three under National Hunt Rules. June Lewis, Guy's mother, rode in point-to-points for ten years – including when she was pregnant with Guy and his twin sister Hannah; among the horses she raced was the gelding Go-Pontinental, who subsequently made a tiny footnote in racing history as one of the finishers in the famous Crisp–Red Rum Grand National of 1973. In a hunter-chase at Chepstow in March 1976 a horse named Boundtobe, trained by Mrs Lewis, was pulled up at the water jump after his saddle slipped. Deciding there was enough energy left in Boundtobe for him to continue his afternoon's exertions elsewhere, she rapidly boxed up the horse at Chepstow and – making a diversion home to pick up her own riding gear – drove him to the point-to-point at nearby Newport, where she arrived in time to declare for the ladies' race. They won. That's the spirit!

By the age of three Guy was riding without the security of either a leading rein or a docile mount: when his 11.2-hand pony Jerry suddenly caught sight of a row of show-jumping obstacles and insisted on carting his infant rider over them, the experience instilled in Guy a love of jumping at speed which has never left him. By the time he was eight he was competing in junior show-jumping and cross-country competitions: for three seasons the twins Guy and Hannah remained unbeaten in pairs events at hunter trials. Later, while still at Monmouth School, he further burnished those skills by spending his holidays riding out at Newmarket for Flat trainer Ben Hanbury and a rather uncomfortable couple of weeks sampling the life of a stable lad at Lambourn with jumps trainer Nicky Henderson. (Among his charges at Nicky Henderson's was the top chaser Mutare, and Guy's stock in the yard was not increased when the horse was found wandering around in the middle of the night. Moral: always check that you've closed the bottom bolt on the box door.)

This sort of thoroughly horsey background made riding second nature for Guy, imbuing him with a complete confidence on and around horses which would stand him in good stead later when he had turned professional: accustomed from an early age to handling and adapting to all sorts of horses, he would be better able to look after himself in the hurly-burly of a novice chase or a twenty-runner handicap hurdle. It also gave him ready access to that somewhat rough-and-tumble school for early race-riding lessons: the point-to-point circuit.

Point-to-point racing – a less formal version of steeple-chasing staged by local hunts, in which all participants are amateurs – has provided the minor league from which so many top jump jockeys have moved on to make their names under Rules. Richard Dunwoody, Peter Scudamore, Adrian

Maguire – most of the modern greats have cut their riding teeth in point-to-points. Guy Lewis first took part in a point-to-point in February 1991, aged sixteen, and rode his first winner (his mother's mare Blinkin' Nora) the following month at the prestigious Beaufort Hunt meeting. His victory on Blinkin' Nora in the members' race at the Llangibby meeting that season maintained a family tradition: his grandfather had won the race in the 1940s, and his father had won it several times, the last occasion being in June 1976 when he beat his wife into second place. In all Guy rode six winners in his first point-to-point season, enough to bring him the Wilkinson Sword Edge Novice Riders' Championship and joint top slot in the Daily Telegraph Novice Riders' Trophy.

This was a career oozing promise – as the pseudonymous point-to-point writer 'Pointsman' noted in an article written late in the 1991 season:

> In the past twenty-four years I have been reporting on the Welsh hunt racing scene I have seen riders like Peter Scudamore, Hywel Davies and Carl Llewellyn graduate from point-to-pointing to National Hunt racing.
>
> But none of them ever impressed me as much as Guy Lewis. If he eventually decided to turn professional, I forecast a successful riding career for this impressive young Gwent rider.

In August that year Guy rode in his first race under Rules (pulled up), and in March 1992, while still at school, hit upon the wheeze of joining the Territorial Army in order to ride a mare named Ketti in the Barclays Bank Hurdle at Sandown Park's Imperial Cup meeting a few days later. Riders in the Barclays Bank Hurdle had to have served in the armed forces: the TA was good enough, and so was the mare, giving Guy Lewis his first winner under Rules – and in a race televised on Channel Four. This was an added bonus, for to ride a winner on television gets the aspiring rider noticed.

Guy was on his way; and what is more, he had already caught the eye of one of the top trainers in the land. Three days after winning on Ketti came a heaven-sent opportunity when Jenny Pitman, who at that stage had trained the winners of two Cheltenham Gold Cups and one Grand National, gave him his first ride at the Cheltenham National Hunt Festival. Strong Gold was only a 20–1 chance in the Fulke Walwyn Kim Muir Challenge Cup, a steeplechase for amateur riders on the opening day of jump racing's most glorious fixture, but ran well to finish fourth after making a bad mistake two fences from home. To have ridden at Cheltenham for the prestigious Mrs Pitman stable was a mark of the regard in which this young jockey – only seventeen – was held.

In February 1993, still an amateur but with his sights now firmly set on a professional career, he rode his first winner of a steeplechase, and in July his first (and only) winner on the Flat, in an amateur riders' race at Salisbury. Later the same year, now aged eighteen, he became stable amateur to trainer Philip Hobbs.

The status of amateur rider over jumps covers a variety of attitudes and aspirations. There are 'genuine' amateurs who have no intention of turning professional, happy to display their talents when they can get the rides. John Oaksey, who rode as John Lawrence before succeeding to his father's title, was one such; Marcus Armytage, who won the Grand National in 1990 on Mr Frisk, another. Both earned their living by journalism. Then there are the young men (and women) on the way up, for whom amateur status is a stepping stone to the professional ranks. The key difference between an amateur and a professional jockey, of course, is that the pro gets paid.

By autumn 1993 Guy Lewis had had enough of riding for nothing. When on 11 November he had four rides at Taunton for zero payment, decision day had arrived. It was time to strike out into the professional ranks, and Guy promptly became a conditional jockey.

The responsibilities of his new status were immediately brought home to him. Riding short-priced favourite Boxing Match at Huntingdon, he let the early leader Tax The Devil get too far in front, and failed to peg him back. As he returned to unsaddle, one disgruntled punter leaned over the rail and shouted out an on-the-spot appraisal of the new professional: 'Lewis, you useless bastard – you should have stayed an amateur!'

Fortunately, not everyone wrote him off so quickly, and the next month he went to work at the Shepton Mallet yard of Paul Nicholls, who was rapidly becoming one of the major trainers in the land.

The category of conditional jockey in National Hunt racing is roughly equivalent to that of an apprentice on the Flat. It denotes a young rider learning his or her craft while formally tied to a particular trainer, and able to claim an 'allowance' – a deduction from the weight which horses they ride must carry – to compensate for the lack of experience of the rider. For a conditional jump jockey at the start of the 1993–4 season, the allowance was seven pounds until he had won fifteen races; then five pounds until he had won thirty races; then three pounds until he had won fifty-five races. Then nothing.

Guy's first winner as a professional came in January 1994, on a horse named Colossus Of Roads in a 'bumper' (a flat race under National Hunt Rules, whose primary purpose is to educate young horses in the ways of racing) on the all-weather track at Lingfield Park. Later the same month he lost his seven-pound claim.

The following month Guy was one of six young jockeys featured in a full-page article in the *Racing Post*. The thrust of the piece was that a number of senior riders were reaching the end of their careers, and 'there is never a shortage of young jockeys eager to fill their boots'. Guy Lewis, described as 'the yuppie conditional', on account of his never being far from his mobile phone, was characterised as having 'the air of the achiever, someone who gets things done'.

So far so good, and more significant landmarks were reached during the 1995–6 term. The five-pound claim went in July 1995, reducing his allowance to three pounds. In March 1996 he had his first ride in the Grand National – an exhilarating circuit and a half on Paul Nicholls's 100–1 shot Brackenfield, still in with a squeak when unseating his rider at the nineteenth fence. Guy may not have turned into the phenomenon of a Tony McCoy – champion for the first time that season having just turned twenty-two, and only six months older than Guy – but he was going the right way: attracting notice, and getting enough rides to make a reasonable living and bankroll the hectic social life which comes with the young jump jockey's territory.

From his first victory under Rules in March 1992, Guy's career had progressed promisingly: just the one winner that season, eight the following season, eleven in 1993–4, back to eight in 1994–5, then up to thirteen in 1995–6 – his best season yet. But the numbers need putting in perspective. Tony McCoy, runaway winner of the jockeys' championship that season, had 759 rides and rode 175 winners, a strike rate of 23 per cent; Guy Lewis's thirteen from 226 rides gave him a strike rate of just 6 per cent. Then again, it is impossible significantly to increase that percentage as long as the vast majority of the horses you are riding have no realistic chance of winning. Fifty-nine jockeys rode more winners than Guy Lewis in the 1995–6 season, which puts him, in the jockeys' own jargon, firmly in 'mid-div'.

But the 1996–7 season promised much. The arrangement with Paul Nicholls seemed to be working out well, and Nicholls's fifty-horse yard would furnish plenty of opportunities for rides when the considerable talents of the stable's regular jockey McCoy were being deployed elsewhere. And there were other trainers apparently keen to use Guy's services, notably Bill Clay, whose yard near Stoke-on-Trent housed a string of around thirty and who for this season would be Guy's 'master', the formal supporter of his application to renew his conditional jockey's licence.

There was also the prospect of losing his three-pound claim. At the beginning of the season Guy had ridden the winners of forty-one races under Rules. The claim would go at fifty-five wins, just fourteen away, and as he had won thirteen races in 1995–6, it was on the cards that this might be his last season claiming any allowance.

Loss of the claim is a serious rite of passage for any jockey, Flat or National Hunt. Suddenly you are on equal terms with more senior riders. If a trainer has the choice between an experienced jockey and an inexperienced conditional, the weight allowance that can be claimed by the conditional may be worth the risk of putting up a more callow rider. Once that distinction has been removed, the inclination will be to plump for experience. So losing the claim tests the young jockey's mettle – and the trainer's faith – to the full.

To get to that point, though, a few more winners had to be chalked up, and it was with great expectations that Guy Lewis went out for his first ride of the new season, Mr Poppleton in a three-mile novices' hurdle at Worcester on Saturday 8 June.

Our hero takes up the story . . .

Mr Poppleton ran respectably enough until running out of steam in the final mile, and then it was a long drive across the country to Southwell for two rides at the evening meeting there, Prince Rockaway in the novice chase and Night Boat – my first ride of the new season for Bill Clay – in the handicap hurdle. Prince Rockaway was tailed off when I pulled him up, and Night Boat never felt like winning, but with three rides it was a reasonable first working day.

One ride at Uttoxeter on the Sunday – Skittle Alley,
tailed off – then nothing until the following Friday
evening at Market Rasen. A nice ride in prospect on my
old favourite Channel Pastime in the handicap chase,
but it all turned very sour: I was fined £250 for
weighing in three pounds heavier than I weighed out.
  Really *pissed off.*

Guy's punishment provided an early-season signal of one element of a jockey's life which can never be ignored: weight.

A constant struggle with the scales is the lot of most riders, famous and obscure alike, and the reason for this near-universal obsession is closely intertwined with the nature of the sport under both National Hunt and Flat codes.

Every horse in every race has to carry – in the form of his jockey and saddle – a specified weight, the precise figure depending on the nature and conditions of the individual race. In the top events – the Cheltenham Gold Cup or Champion Hurdle, say, or the Derby on the Flat – all the runners carry the same weight, so the best horse on the day should win. (An allowance is made for mares and fillies to reflect their supposed relative weakness.) But if every race were won by the best horse in the field, the sport would soon become uncompetitive, and – crucially – not much of a betting medium. To make matters more interesting, and give lesser horses a chance of winning races, the idea of the handicap was introduced as far back as the eighteenth century. In a handicap the weights to be carried by individual horses are adjusted – better horses carrying more than the less good – so that in theory their chances are equalised.

As for the amount of difference weight is supposed to make to the performance of an individual horse, according to form experts a pound in weight, in a hurdle or steeplechase, is approximately equivalent to a length in distance. By this theory, if horse A and horse B carry the same weight in a race and horse A wins by one length, they will dead-heat if that race is re-run under identical conditions with horse A carrying one pound more than horse B. Rarely do matters work out that precisely, and a number of factors mitigate the effect of weight: a big horse, for example, will feel variations of weight less than a small horse.

The weight range in Flat races is roughly between seven stone and ten stone (colts in the Derby, for example, carry nine stone, fillies eight stone nine pounds), and to make a reasonable living the average Flat jockey will need to be able to 'do' eight stone or less on a regular basis. Hence the collection of diminutive figures seen scuttling into the paddock at Newmarket or Goodwood. Jump racing, with its roots in the hunting field and its (for the most part) older, stronger horses, has a higher range of weights – roughly between ten and twelve stone.

Whether on the Flat or under National Hunt Rules, it is imperative for a jockey to be able to maintain his weight at a level which combines the strength to control and drive three-quarters of a ton of racehorse with the lightness which will bring rides his way. The lighter you are, the more rides you will get, since there are more bad horses in training than good ones, and the bad ones carry the lower weights in handicaps. A jump jockey who could not do under eleven stone would be severely restricted in his opportunities. Yet force yourself to be too light and you will also be too weak.

The effort of keeping weight down has led to famous cases of deprivation. Lester Piggott was tall for a Flat jockey, but sheer determination and a spartan lifestyle kept his body at roughly two stone below his natural weight throughout his riding life: his minimum riding weight for most of his career was eight stone five pounds, including clothing and saddle. Fred Archer, the greatest jockey of the nineteenth century, would lose weight by imbibing a fearsome laxative which became known as 'Archer's Mixture'. ('I tried it myself when I was riding races,' wrote the famous trainer George Lambton, 'and from my own experience I should say it was made of dynamite.') But in Archer's case the necessity to keep his weight low became, literally, a matter of life and death. In October 1886 he was riding St Mirrin in the Cambridgeshire at Newmarket, and despite fierce wasting put up one pound overweight. That one pound proved crucial, for St Mirrin was beaten a head. Archer's wasting brought on a fever, and although he had a few more rides, early the following month he shot himself in a fit of delirium.

Given the higher range of weights, jump jockeys tend to have it easier than their Flat counterparts, but meeting the demands of the scales is still a struggle for many, and ways of winning it – some within the rules, some not – are legion.

The simplest, of course, is rigidly to control your diet, to avoid fatty foods and limit your intake of fluids. The latter course is a particularly unappealing one to most jump jockeys, for whom the night out is part and parcel of their calling, but alcohol is fattening. (Wine is often the preferred tipple of jockeys – less fluid than beer, therefore less immediate weight gain.) So try not to eat and drink; but if you really must, the standard remedy is to sweat off the effects of that intake in a sauna (most racecourses now have a sauna in the weighing room). Some jockeys take laxatives, some go running in a sweatsuit. (Early in his career Lester Piggott, even on the hottest day, would drive to the races wearing a sweatsuit, with the car's heater going full blast. The pounds rolled off him, but the habit tended to deprive him of the company of fellow jockeys who might have shared the cost of the petrol.)

For Guy Lewis, keeping to his minimum riding weight is a constant battle. Which brings us back to Market Rasen . . .

If a horse is down to carry ten stone in a handicap, my three-pound claim brings the weight down to nine stone eleven. Silks, breeches, boots and the saddle made up with stirrup leathers, irons and girths come to about three pounds, so to ride at nine eleven I need to weigh nine eight stripped, which with enough warning and the odd bout in the sauna I can usually do –though other factors affect your weight: it's harder to lose those last few pounds when you have a cold, for instance.

At Market Rasen I had to do nine eleven, as Channel Pastime had ten stone in the race, less my three-pound allowance. It's never easy to do your minimum, and I knew I'd be struggling to do the weight. If you absolutely can't do it you can declare overweight, but this does not endear you to trainers who have booked you on the understanding that the weight is within your capabilities.

The normal procedure of weighing out is that you present yourself to the Clerk of the Scales, who sits just outside the changing room checking jockeys on and off the scales. You are allowed a pound for the weight of the body protector which all jockeys have to wear (so if your horse is down to carry ten stone, you will actually be weighed at ten one), and there are various bits of equipment which you don't take on the scales with you: crash helmet and cap, whip, breast girth, number cloth. You sit on the scales, are passed as having the correct weight by the Clerk, then hand your saddle to the horse's trainer, who is waiting as you come off the scales.

Simple – but there are ways of cheating.

That day I'd been in the sauna for what felt like hours but was still not light enough, so I borrowed a pair of 'cheating boots' from another jockey. This is a pair of boots so light and thin that it would be too painful on the feet to ride in them, but to all other intents and purposes – and to the Clerk of the Scales – they look like ordinary riding boots. Ironically, I had on me a pair of real boots no heavier than those, a pair in which I could just about ride comfortably, but decided that to be on the safe side I'd better use the cheating boots.

So I weighed out wearing the other lad's cheating boots, and no body protector – or rather, a false body protector, one from which the pads, the bits that actually do the protecting, had been removed. Someone glancing at me would have seen the outline of a body protector under my silks, but there was no protection.

I weighed out – nine twelve on the scales, nine eleven in the Clerk's book having taken off the pound allowance for the (assumed) back protector – and gave the saddle to trainer Dai Burchell. I then went back into the changing room, put my own light boots on and changed into my (real) body protector. You're not supposed to do this – though plenty of jockeys would do so in a similar situation.

Dehydrated from all the time in the course sauna, I allowed myself the luxury of a cup of tea in the changing room before going out for the race. This was racing in the height of summer, and I thought I was bound to lose at least half a pound from the effort of riding, so I reasoned that a cup of tea would do no harm.

Then I went out for the race, in which Channel Pastime plodded on at one pace to finish fourth.

The number of jockeys who have to weigh in after a race is at the discretion of the Clerk of the Scales – it can be all riders in the race, or only those on the placed horses – and on this occasion the instruction was: first four weigh. I got on to the scales: just over two pounds heavy.

The Clerk of the Scales queried my boots.

'They're the same pair,' I claimed, but he insisted that by being over two pounds heavy I was a case for the stewards, and off he went to tell them. It was like being sneaked on at school.

I went in before the stewards' panel and pleaded my case: I'd struggled to do the weight, it was hot weather,

I'd had a drink, I assumed I'd lose weight during the race, otherwise I'd have put up a pound overweight.

They were unimpressed by my eloquence, and fined me £250 – which about wiped out my profit for the season so far.

The following day I was riding at the course again, and the Clerk went out of his way to be nice. 'No hard feelings, Guy,' he insisted – and I suppose there weren't.

I had nine eleven to do that day too, and made certain I did it properly. Finished nowhere. I came in after the race and didn't have to weigh in, but just to prove my point sat on the scales. No problem. What a waste of £250!

Jockeys weigh in overweight all the time, and often the Clerk of the Scales will turn a blind eye to a marginal case. And sometimes our excuses are more plausible than others. In the days when there were jump races on the artificial all-weather surfaces I was riding in a hurdle on the Equitrack at Lingfield Park. I was doing eleven stone, and wearing woollies, not silks. It was pissing down with rain, and after finishing third I came back to weigh in covered from top to toe in sand. My woolly jumper was saturated with rain, I had sand stuck all over me – and when I weighed in I was six pounds overweight. The Clerk raised an eyebrow, but when I pointed out the circumstances he let me through.

The real irony behind all this agonising over weight all the time is that the odd pound on or off his back is

going to make very little difference to a strapping great
steeplechaser. On the Flat, two or three pounds might
make a difference to a horse, especially in a competitive
race like a sprint handicap, but to most jumping horses
a pound or two would be like the touch of a finger on a
man's back.

One week into Guy Lewis's season: five rides, from which
one fourth place, three unplaced, one pulled up; and a fine of
£250.

Things can only get better.

3

———

Off the Mark

'My gran could have won on him'

UNPLACED, UNPLACED, UNPLACED, PULLED UP, pulled up: Guy's next five rides did little to dispel the frustration of a low-key start. To go into a race with at least a squeak of a chance would have made a change, but there's not much likelihood of that when you're riding rubbish horses, and until you start working your way up the hierarchy of skill and experience there are going to be plenty of those.

Jump jockeys, so the conventional wisdom goes, form a close-knit family of sportsmen and sportswomen, fabled for their camaraderie. Like many another group of individuals bonded by a common purpose – and especially a common danger – they readily invest their colleagues with nicknames, though not always the ones the press would have us adopt. The papers may insist that Richard Dunwoody is known as 'The Prince' to his weighing-room colleagues, but you will rarely if ever hear him addressed as that: 'Woody' is his name. Adrian Maguire's nickname is 'Mutley'; Robert Thornton's is 'Chocolate' (not, apparently, because he shares his surname with a manufacturer of the stuff, but because of his own predilection for it); Jason Titley's you may work out for yourself. Some, such as 'Leg Lock' for Luke Harvey, gain currency from their bearers' riding style. More mundane are the ones based on initials: Tony McCoy, for instance, attracts nothing more exotic or cryptic than 'AP'; Brendan Powell is 'BP'. Others are more obscure: Rodney Farrant is 'Pigeon', Ian Lawrence is 'Marmite'. If Guy Lewis himself has a nickname in the weighing room, he will not reveal what it is.

Yet there is a strict hierarchy among the jockeys – none the less firmly established for being unspoken – which is nowhere better expressed than in the strict convention decreeing who has which peg in the racecourse changing room.

This pecking order is firmly controlled by the senior valets on duty at the course that day, each of whom will, within his patch in the changing room, rank his riders according to a formula based on a mixture of length of service and individual eminence. Richard Dunwoody, who registers high on both counts but was not, in the 1996–7 season, the reigning champion, has undisputed claim to pole position; Brendan Powell takes precedence over Tony McCoy on grounds of seniority. Jockeys often like to base themselves at the same peg from which they have won big races: Richard Guest, for example, has an understandable preference for the place in the Cheltenham changing room from which he went out to ride Beech Road to victory in the 1989 Champion Hurdle. (At some of the major courses, big-race wins are permanently commemorated at the pegs.) A seven-pound claiming conditional jockey would start somewhere over near the toilets and gradually work his way up the order. Thus an aspiring rider can plot his progress through the ranks, and Guy wishes he were further along than he is. But he knows his place.

And whether you are the reigning champion or a rookie conditional, whether the object of your professional services is a useless novice hurdler or a potential Gold Cup winner, whether you are a star in the jumping firmament wondering about your next appearance on *A Question of Sport* or a struggling journeyman wondering about your next riding fee, the routine for a day at the races remains basically the same.

If Guy knows, from weighing himself first thing in the morning, that he needs to sweat off a few pounds in order to do his lightest weight of the day, he aims to arrive at the racecourse a couple of hours before his first ride in order to get down to the required weight in the sauna – or, if there's no sauna (not all racecourses have one) by putting on a bin liner and going for a run. If there are no excess pounds to be shed, arrival will be about an hour before. (A jockey *must* have registered his arrival at the course at least fifteen minutes before the off-time of the first race in which he is riding. Miss that deadline and the trainer will have found another rider.)

Guy takes with him his basic riding equipment:

* Four racing saddles (a very minimalist distant relative of the usual saddle seen on the back of your average riding-school hack) of varying sizes – and therefore varying weights, and varying

levels of comfort. The smallest weighs just half a pound, which helps when he's trying to 'do light' but provides an uncomfortable seat on the back of a large, wide-backed chaser. When that saddle is 'made up' – when it has girths and stirrup leathers and aluminium irons attached – it will weigh about one and a half pounds. His other saddles weigh three pounds, six pounds, and – the luxury of riding at a high weight! – nine pounds.

* His body protector, a compulsory piece of equipment for all jockeys, Flat or jumping: a sort of neck-high waistcoat which zips down the middle. Protection is afforded by the slabs of foam rubber sewn into pockets all over the front and back.

* His skull cap – a specialised form of crash helmet – the design of which has to meet strict Jockey Club specifications. The helmet itself is made of fibreglass and is kept in place by a face harness, webbing straps which secure under the chin. The shell of the helmet is designed to absorb the energy of any impact by partially destructing, so once a skull cap has been severely knocked it must be discarded.

* Whips, which likewise must meet strict Jockey Club specifications (maximum length 68 centimetres, minimum diameter 1 centimetre, flap to be covered in felt, etc.).

* Pairs of goggles. Most jockeys will wear two – even three – pairs of goggles during a race under

muddy conditions, pulling off the top pair as they get covered with mud.

* Pairs of riding boots, of differing weights: the lightest three-quarters of a pound, the heaviest two pounds.

One of the most important persons in Guy's – and any jockey's – riding life is his valet.

The jockey's valet – pronounce the word 'vallett' in racing circles – is the ultimate backroom boy, without whose unsung efforts in preparing the jockeys for every ride the sport could not run smoothly, and for whose services jockeys pay a percentage of each riding fee. A combination of nursemaid, washerwoman and personal assistant, the jockey's valet transports clothing and equipment from meeting to meeting, laying it out in readiness before the jockeys arrive and washing it after they have departed. But that is only part of the job, in addition to which valets provide all sorts of informal assistance to their charges, services that can be especially crucial for a jump jockey after a fall: in that event, it is usually the rider's valet who will make arrangements about the jockey's car, answer calls on the mobile phone, see that a stricken rider can get home. Whatever needs doing, he'll do it.

Best known of the fifteen valets working in British racing is John Buckingham, immortalised in racing history as the jockey who rode 100–1 outsider Foinavon to sensational victory in the 1967 Grand National after most of the field had been brought to a standstill by a pile-up at the twenty-third fence. He became a valet following his retirement from the saddle in 1971, and now works in partnership with his brother Tom.

So by the time Guy has selected from the boot of his car the particular versions of his equipment he will need for that day, shoved them into his riding bag and made for the weighing room, his valet will have arranged by his peg in the changing room his riding clothes: the colours, which have been brought to the course by the horse's trainer; a white polo-neck shirt to be worn under those colours; breeches; and – to some outsiders a bizarre accoutrement for participants in this most daredevil of sports – a couple of pairs of ladies' tights. Far from furnishing evidence of closet transvestism, tights provide jockeys with an ideal combination of warmth, lightness and protection from chafing underneath their breeches. (Weighing-room lore insists that a jockey desperate to save every fraction of an ounce before weighing out has requested tights of a lower denier.)

An early – and essential – race-day obligation for a jockey is to present his medical book to the Declarations Clerk. The medical book is his passport, without which he cannot ride, and contains details of all injuries in action which have required medical attention. If, in the opinion of the racecourse doctor, a jockey is unfit to ride following an injury, the doctor signs the book in red. As soon as that injury is considered cured, the annotation 'Fit to ride' is entered in black or blue, again by a course medical officer, and the jockey can get back into the thick of things: hence the jargon of getting 'signed off'. At the beginning of the 1996–7 season, the last red entry in Guy's book was dated 1 November 1995 and read: 'Bruised thigh – not to ride until passed by RMO.' Three days later the RMO – Racecourse Medical Officer – had signed him back on again in black.

Guy gets changed, then weighs himself holding the tack with which in a few moments he will be officially weighed out. If even with his heaviest saddle and boots he is too light, a leather weight cloth is added, to be placed on the horse's back under the saddle: this cloth contains pockets into which half-pound or one-pound strips of lead can be inserted until the requisite weight is made up.

About half an hour before the first race in which he is engaged, he weighs out on the scales opposite a table at which sits the Clerk of the Scales. He does not weigh out with his skull cap or whip (so you can't cheat by using a weighted whip, nor take an additional risk by wearing a flimsy skull cap), breast girth or number cloth. The trainer of the horse he is about to ride is waiting as the jockey comes off the scales, whereupon he takes the saddle and goes off to tack up the horse, leaving Guy to return to the weighing room for a cup of tea or a smoke or a few minutes' doze. Or, as we saw at Market Rasen, an illicit quick change . . .

When the signal is made for the jockeys to be ready, coloured silk caps are stretched over crash helmets and tied in place by the valet; then comes the call into the parade ring. Here each will be greeted by the horse's trainer and (usually) owner, who will dispense instructions about how their charge should be ridden. A fly on the wall (or on the paddock rail) buzzing around to eavesdrop might find the wording of such conversations baffling – 'Drop him in . . . Pop him out and make it . . . Don't disappoint him' – even more so when they may seem to contradict the very point of a race: 'Don't win too far' (connections do not want the horse to appear so superior to his rivals that his weight in future handicaps goes too high for him to win again) or 'He's not expected today, but we'll look after you when he is.' (There is an apocryphal tale of an innocent young jockey called before the stewards after making no visible effort to win his race. 'What were your instructions?' the stewards ask him. He replies: 'I was told to wait.' The stewards ask: 'How long were you told to wait?' 'Until Chepstow next week.')

A few minutes after the jockeys have entered the parade ring and received their instructions, the signal is given to mount. Often this is the first time that the jockey has ever sat on this particular horse, and in such circumstances he will be alert for the early impressions that are often eloquent of the horse's physical and temperamental characteristics. Now is the time to adjust the length of stirrup leathers to suit that horse's physique, and often, especially if he has not ridden the horse before, to receive from the stable lad or lass leading the horse round a more informal but more accurate assessment of the horse's chances than it would have been politic for the trainer to offer in the presence of the owner: 'He pulls like buggery . . . He jumps to the right . . . He's not fit.'

The canter down to the start is a telling time. In this couple of minutes a jockey will learn a great deal about an unfamiliar horse – how he uses himself, how co-ordinated he feels – and even from the canter can form a reasonable opinion about how that horse will jump.

It is common practice for jump jockeys to take their horses up to look at the first fence or first hurdle. Whether or not this instils in the horse a sense of what he is about to be required to do, or whether he thinks of it as nothing more than looking over the garden hedge, jockeys tend to like that routine.

Canter back to the start, and have the girth checked. The girth is likely to need tightening after that initial canter, since the horse may blow itself out when the saddle is first put on, and going through the faster paces on the way to the start may loosen the saddle's moorings.

Walk the horse round with the others. Then, when the starter is satisfied that all is in order and the appointed time for the start has been reached, he calls the runners into line. Races under National Hunt Rules are not dispatched from starting stalls, nor is there a draw to determine which horse starts from which position across the track, so the start can be a difficult moment for a jockey trying to get his wayward mount off with the other runners and in the place he wants. The position you take up may depend on the horse – for example, on an inexperienced jumper you might not want to start on the inside, where there tend to be greater traffic problems than on the outer. As television microphones now testify, in the few moments before the start the air is often blue with jockeys importuning the starter either not to let the runners go as their horses are facing the wrong way – 'No, sir! No, sir! No, sir!' – or to send them off without any further delay. (Before the 1996 John Hughes Memorial Trophy at Aintree, in which Guy Lewis enjoyed an exhilarating round on Channel Pastime, David Bridgwater was memorably picked up by the microphone exhorting the starter: 'Let 'em go, sir – mine's shitting 'imself!')

After the race the first four horses home will be unsaddled in the winner's enclosure; those unplaced are attended to away from the hubbub, and for the jockey of a beaten horse this part of the afternoon's activity requires skills every bit as nifty as presenting your horse at a fence at thirty miles an hour. According to Guy Lewis, half the jockey's job is about riding the horse; the other half is public relations, and during the post-race discussion with the trainer and (especially) the owner those PR skills can be tested to their limits.

No racehorse owner likes to hear the dreadful truth that his or her horse is no good. Statistics tell them that only one in three horses in training ever wins a race, but the essence of ownership is that your horse will be that one – if not in this race, then next time for sure. The jockey, dismounting from his steaming partner, has to keep that hope alive if he wants any chance of continuing to ride for that owner; so the horse is 'game as a pebble' even though he finished a furlong behind his rivals; needs a longer trip; needs a shorter trip; needs time (always a useful standby); needs blinkers; needs a right-handed track; needs a left-handed track; needs a stiffer track; needs a rest. (But *never* that suggestion jockeys are sometimes tempted to offer: needs a bullet.)

Having dispensed appreciation of the horse's efforts to winning owners or soothing balm to beaten owners, the jockey returns to the weighing room. Normally only the riders of placed horses are required to be weighed, but this is at the discretion of the Clerk of the Scales, who can if he chooses weigh everyone who finishes, even in a very big field.

If the jockey has another ride that day, the colours will be waiting, and the process is repeated. If that was his last (or only) ride of the day, he changes back into his civilian clothes, packs his riding bag and leaves the rest of his gear with his valet, who will wash it and have it ready for him wherever he is riding next.

Quick shower, then out to the car – or the bar.

Race-day routine forms only one part – albeit the most public part – of the professional jockey's life. Another major stipulation in the job description is that almost every day the jockey rise at the crack of dawn, and sometimes much earlier, to squint bleary-eyed through the windscreen as he drives to a trainer to 'ride out' – that is, give the horses their morning exercise. The horses will usually go out in two or more batches – 'lots' – and a jockey may be called on to ride in just one 'lot' or to take part in them all. Occasionally riding out will be supplemented by 'riding work' – galloping a horse seriously to see what he is capable of – and 'schooling' – putting a horse over obstacles to teach him to jump, or give him a refresher course in the finer points.

A few years ago the Injured Jockeys' Fund Christmas card neatly summed up the extremes of riding out with two paintings depicting a string of racehorses in the morning: 'Absolute Heaven', when the sun was shining, the birds were (presumably) singing, and all was right with the world; and 'Absolute Hell', when the wind was gusting, the rain was lashing, and horses and humans were joined in the misery of what they had to do.

For Guy, as for all jockeys, riding out is an essential part of the job.

Most times a trainer will expect you to come and ride a horse you're going to partner in a race – at least ride him out, if possible school him over a few hurdles or fences. (Richard Davis went to Laura Shally's yard to school Mr Sox a few days before the accident, but was not able to pop the horse over a couple of fences as the ground was too hard.)

Different trainers have different methods. Some, if they have a horse who's never even seen a hurdle before, put him over a little pole a few times to see how he uses himself. Some horses are not natural jumpers while others take to it, but most will sort themselves out if left alone, and many trainers like to try their horses in an indoor school without a rider, lungeing each one over a pole or a hurdle so that he can learn to cope for himself.

Trainers have hurdles and fences on their gallops, and when a horse is ready he will be schooled over these, usually scaled-down versions of the real thing.

Normally horses school over fences or hurdles in pairs, either upsides or with the more experienced horse giving the less experienced a lead to show him what to do. But some horses will not school. Kadari, whom I've ridden a good few times and on whom I've won three races, would not jump a blade of grass at home, and would just jam on the brakes coming to the schooling fence.

It always helps (though it's not always possible) to know in advance of a race how your horse jumps, and when you don't think a horse has been schooled properly, that can give you some very hairy moments.

But when you have confidence in your horse, the whole business is a lot simpler, and it's so much easier

*to see a stride when you're confident that your horse
will understand what you're telling him. You can
normally see a stride five or six actual strides before the
fence, then ask your horse to lengthen into it, making
him stride out that tiny bit extra so that he's in exactly
the right place to take off; or if you want to go short,
you take a pull out of his mouth and lean back a little:
you can be back up his neck in another stride, ready
for take-off. Always the knack is seeing the stride early
enough, though some horses are best left to the last
minute. The worst sort of jumper of fences is the horse
who can't or won't go short when asked, and then
can't get higher than the guard rail on the take-off side
of the fence. It's on that sort that you really start
shitting yourself.*

The end of June 1996 brought a welcome interruption to
Guy's routine and a rare perk – albeit one which he would
have to finance himself – in the form of a trip to the Czech
Republic.

Jump jockeys have less opportunity for regular overseas
travel than their counterparts on the Flat. A top Flat jockey
such as Frankie Dettori will, for most of the year, jet around
between Britain, Ireland, France, Italy and the USA, with visits
to Dubai, Japan, South Africa, Australia and Hong Kong also
in the itinerary. A top jump jockey will ride regularly in
Ireland, occasionally in France, and sporadically in the USA.

For the journeyman such as Guy Lewis such trips are few
and far between, so the chance to ride in the Czech Republic
at the famous course of Pardubice – where the Velka

Pardubicka, the Czech equivalent of the Grand National, is staged in October – was one not to be missed.

The trip was organised through racing artists Dave and Adrian Dent, and four jockeys went out from Britain to ride at the meeting which features the Czech Gold Cup: Richard Davis, Chris Maude, Keith Dempsey and myself. It was of course a serious venture forging links between British and Czech racing, and all that sort of thing, but not surprisingly it turned into a great lads' holiday.

Beforehand we were all a bit dubious about the whole enterprise: we didn't know what kind of country it was – in fact any impression we had of the country was of its former Communist incarnation, Czechoslovakia. We expected something pretty grim and had a few drinks on the plane on the way out to fortify ourselves; but on arrival we discovered just how wrong we'd been.

We arrived in Pardubice late at night, were met by the Czech people who were looking after us on the trip, and checked into our hotel. Soon after sitting down in the hotel restaurant, which seemed to double up as a night club, a group of young girls came over and insisted on sitting down with us – and, before long, on our laps. They turned out to be local prostitutes, but, all being clean-living lads, we made our excuses and retired for the night.

The race meeting took place over two days, but we were riding only on day one. First into action was

Chris Maude, who rode in a chase and finished third. Next off was myself, on a horse with the glamorous name of Sinus. This race was over the cross-country course, which twists and turns all over the place: just walking the course in the morning made me feel dizzy. Richard was due to ride over the same course later in the afternoon, and spent at least two hours walking round the track, memorising the route: in the end his horse didn't run in that race, so all his preparation was wasted!

Sinus had already won three races, and I was assured that he could win this, but after about a mile he started to backtrack, and finished fifth.

All four of us visiting jockeys had a ride in the Czech Gold Cup, run not over the cross-country track but over the more orthodox steeplechase course (not unlike our point-to-point circuits). I rode a mare named Starting Order. Connections were raving about her chances, and she was well fancied, but when I put her over the practice fence on the way to the start she tried to jam on the brakes and only just managed to jump it, which didn't do much for my confidence, however good her chances were supposed to be.

The weather had got steadily worse as we left the paddock, and by the time we got to the start it was absolutely bucketing down with rain – I've never ridden in conditions like it. The start was delayed until the weather had settled, and as we were walking our horses round we were getting wetter and wetter, moaning and groaning to each other. Our boots were filling up with water and none of us was wearing waterproofs. It was miserable! Eventually the starter let us go, and things got even worse: the kickback from all the mud was horrendous, and as the weather had been OK when we went out to ride I was wearing only one pair of goggles, which very soon became useless.

My mare hated every minute of it, and was never going a yard, but at least I fared better than Chris Maude: I was upsides him at a ditch when I saw him tumble off. I pulled up before the second last, Keith Dempsey finished seventh, and Richard's horse ran fourth.

After that race the other lads were finished for the day, but I had one more ride to go, a horse named Varadero. He was a great big nutty seven-year-old, seventeen hands high, and hadn't raced for ages – though they told me he'd been show jumping! He tried to run away with me going down to the start, but in the race itself ran well, jumping like a stag. He felt as if he would stay for ever, so throughout the last half mile I kept after him. There are no rules about use of the whip in the Czech Republic so I didn't have to worry about a bollocking from the stewards, and throughout the last half mile I didn't put my stick down. Turning into the straight we were fourth, and I drove Varadero all the way to the line. We passed the third horse and the second and were rapidly closing down on the leader, but just failed to get up and were beaten a neck.

All the lads were watching in the stand and madly cheering me on, and though I hadn't won we got a great reception as we came back in. Varadero's owners were as chuffed as beans, and said I could come back and ride their horse in the Velka Pardubicka itself in October.

If the racing was incident-packed, so was the night life. One night Chris Maude had taken to his bed with a bout of Czech tummy and Richard and I went out to a club. When we got back to our hotel Richard went off to bed and I sat in the foyer having what I thought would be my last drink of the evening when a waiter came over and started engaging me in conversation. This was rather difficult as he couldn't speak English, but we passed a merry half an hour or so before he suggested I go to his room for a few more drinks. There we were joined by a couple of extremely good-looking girls who turned out to be cleaners in the hotel. After a session in that room we moved across to mine to raid the mini-bar, and were joined there by Dave Dent and the others.

They had been in the hotel's other 'night club', which turned out to have been the local brothel! There was a huge bouncer on the door who, they reported, looked like Meatloaf, and once they'd gone in they were worried that this man mountain might not be too impressed if they were to leave without at least dabbling in the usual business of a brothel. They decided to pool their resources. Exactly what happened then is unclear, but one of their group disappeared for about an hour . . .

Another evening I was sitting in the foyer late on when all of a sudden I was surrounded by a horde of *about fifteen big, beefy, mustachioed Polish airmen, each with a bottle of brandy in his hand. Although they couldn't speak English and I couldn't work out what they were trying to say to me, one thing was clear enough: I was to join them for a drink, and before I knew it I was downing brandy diluted – if that's the word – with Bailey's Irish Cream, a really rancid cocktail. I told them that I was a professional jockey but they didn't seem to understand that, so I assured them that I was a fighter pilot – which really struck a chord with them. Every time I insisted I had to go up to bed they insisted that I have one more drink with them, and I started to think I'd never get away. But real alarm set in when I heard one of them call me 'Pretty Boy'. I thought: Oh my God! – here I am with a bunch of Polish airmen about to take out their frustration on an innocent, blond, blue-eyed boy from Britain. I was beginning to get seriously worried when Dave Dent turned up and rescued me, whisking me away from my new friends and – very much the worse for the brandy and Bailey's – back to my room.*

At a dinner on our last evening, our translator Lucie Sediva gave a speech: 'This week a little piece of England came to Pardubicka . . . and things here will never be the same.'

Back home, there was a faint hint of better times ahead when Channel Pastime was runner-up in a good handicap chase at Market Rasen early in July, but after that the supply of rides seemed to dry up.

Then came Friday 19 July: the day Richard Davis rode Mr Sox at Southwell.

I'd seen Richard a few times during the week after we'd come back from the Czech trip, but had then gone abroad on holiday for a week. My twin sister Hannah was getting married to the trainer Nick Walker on the Saturday, and on the Friday I was in Newport on a last-minute shopping trip to buy a few things for my mother for the wedding. A horse named Noblely, trained by Nick, was running in the second at Southwell that afternoon, so I went into a betting shop to watch the race, and noticed as the runners were coming out on to the course that the camera was showing a stretcher being eased into an ambulance. It was a very hot day, and at first I assumed that the ambulance must have been for some old chap who'd passed out because of the heat: I just didn't think anything of it at the time, and watched Noblely's race.

A few minutes later I got a call on my mobile phone from my other sister Zoë, Richard's girlfriend: Richard's had a bad fall. As I was driving home she phoned again: Richard's critical. I got back home at about four o'clock and found Zoë in tears: Richard was still critical in hospital in Nottingham, and she had to go up there. In the event we decided it would be best if my uncle – who was visiting for the wedding – took her up. Three hours later she phoned from the hospital to say that Richard had died.

I'd known Richard a long time, and had got much closer to him during the Czech trip. My first reaction was one of sheer disbelief. After a couple of hours I'd calmed down and the initial shock had started to wear off, and I found myself thinking about fate: when your time's up, your time's up.

I was supposed to be meeting Nick Walker and his family at the Stakis Hotel near our farm, and knew that I had to get there quick in order to tell them what had happened: they couldn't be allowed to find out from the news or some other way. At the hotel I took Nick to one side and told him, and the rest of that evening is mostly a blur.

On the Saturday the wedding went ahead, though what had happened the day before obviously cast a long shadow: Richard would have been there. The day after the wedding was when it really began to sink in, and that Sunday we spent hours sitting around talking about what had happened.

As far as race riding was concerned, it simply never crossed my mind that what happened to Richard would affect my attitude towards my job. Of course what happened to him could have happened to me, could happen to me on my next ride, but it wasn't something to dwell on. If Richard hadn't ridden Mr Sox, someone else would have. I'd lost a friend – I'd never had anyone that close to me die before – and how he died didn't really matter. I'd have ridden the next day without a second thought. My bottle wasn't affected at all.

The funeral was very upsetting, especially upsetting when 'American Pie' was played during the service. Richard knew every word of that song, and I must have heard him sing it dozens of times. Wherever we went, if there was a karaoke machine, up he'd get and sing 'American Pie'. One night on that trip to the Czech Republic we were in a night club where there was a little band – organ and guitar – playing horrendous music. When the musicians went off for their break, Richard got up on the stage and, unaccompanied, starting singing 'American Pie': the rest of us were all cringing in our seats, but it sent a shiver down our spines when we heard it again at the funeral.

I was riding the day after, and although the other jockeys went off to The Plough, I didn't feel I wanted to go and get drunk with them. In my head, I'd already had my own little funeral for Richard, already said goodbye to him.

Channel Pastime had been due to run at Stratford on the Sunday after Richard's death and I'd have ridden him as usual, but his trainer Dai Burchell had forgotten to declare him on the Friday morning. In any case, his owners Sandra and Mel Worthington, who knew Richard and had put him up on the horse when I couldn't ride him, said that in the circumstances he wouldn't have run Channel Pastime at Stratford anyway.

Guy's ride on Channel Pastime on the day after Richard Davis's funeral was the third time he'd ridden the horse this season, and the twenty-fourth outing for the partnership under Rules, in addition to their eight races (three wins) in point-to-points. So Channel Pastime was a horse high in his jockey's affections.

A jockey cannot become fond of every horse he rides, but most of us have one particular horse who has helped us on our way when we're setting out – and for me Channel Pastime was just such a horse. I won three point-to-points on him very early on and had ridden him many times under Rules. In March 1996 he gave me my first experience over the Grand National fences at Aintree, starting at 200–1 in the John Hughes Memorial Trophy but running a wonderful race. It was the first time round Aintree for both of us, and I think he worried himself a little early on, but when he got the hang of the fences he was just superb – he absolutely flew the Canal Turn – and was still in contention coming back across the Melling Road and fourth jumping the last, before fading a little up the run-in. What a thrill!

The following month we won a chase at Ludlow by a neck – his first win under Rules. In October 1994 I'd been stood down for two days due to concussion, and had to miss riding the horse in a race at Wincanton: my place was taken by Richard.

Channel Pastime's owners Mel and Sandra Worthington are close friends of my family and of Richard's parents, so it was fitting that my first ride after his death should be on the horse. Indeed, Sandra

*specifically asked me if I could make Channel Pastime
my first ride after Richard's accident.*

*In the month after Richard's death I found myself
conscious of some of the dodgy horses I was having to
ride, many of them suffering from the same problem –
that they got so revved up they became really
dangerous. When you get one in that mood there's not
an awful lot you can do.*

*Early in August there was Galloping Guns at
Newton Abbot – a horse I'd known to be a bit of a
tearaway in the past, though he was OK that day.
Not OK was my other ride the same afternoon,
Late Encounter in the bumper: he dumped me on
the way to the start.*

*At Stratford later that month I had two rides and
they were both 100–1 shots. One was Galloping Guns,
a 100–1 chance if ever I saw one, and the other was
Athenian Alliance, a horse I rode as others didn't want
to: last time out she'd run away with her jockey going
down to the start at Worcester – did two circuits before
running out of puff!*

*At Stratford I dropped her in and got her home, but
she still blew up.*

'I dropped her in and got her home, but she still blew up.'
Jump racing, like all sports, has its own language, and jump
jockeys speak a particular kind of argot. Their reportage of a
race is peppered with familiar words and phrases used in (to
outsiders) unfamiliar ways. When a horse is 'travelling' he is
running comfortably, or 'well within himself'. 'On the bridle'

has much the same meaning, while 'off the bridle' indicates the opposite – that the horse is having to be pushed along by his rider. 'Scrubbed along' is a neatly graphic way of describing the same condition (imagine someone scrubbing the back step with both hands).

A horse has 'pinged' a fence if he jumps it quickly and cleanly; has 'pecked' if his head nods towards the ground on landing; has 'put down' if he fails to take off on the stride his jockey asks him to; has 'come up out of my hands' if he takes off of his own accord before his rider gives him a signal; and, with the euphemism characteristic of jockey jargon, may be 'going down a bit free' on the way to post if he seems to be disposed to break the world land speed record.

But in addition to quirks of vocabulary, there is a distinctive jockey's way of phrasing. Often a jump jockey describing a race will add a layer of immediacy to the account by speaking in the perfect tense: 'He's pinged the first, put down at the second, then he's jumped from fence to fence. But he's blown up after three out.'

Guy reeled off the sentence 'At Stratford I dropped her in and got her home, but she still blew up' with the ease of habitual practice. Only an outsider would need the explanation that during the Stratford race he put the mare in behind other runners rather than let her make the pace, and thus preserved enough of her energy to enable her to complete the course. But she still ran out of breath.

As the peculiar language of jockeyship indicates, there are many ways of riding horses. Some horses like to race in front of their rivals, others need holding up until the last possible second, as they will stop – or to be more accurate, stop racing and start to ease off – once they are in front. A familiar example of the former was Desert Orchid, whose customary (though not invariable) way of racing was to try to dominate his rivals by making most or all of the running. And as a familiar example of the latter we could cite Miinnehoma, on whom Richard Dunwoody famously 'took a pull' (restrained the horse) halfway up the run-in of the 1994 Grand National: National or no National, Miinnehoma could not be allowed to strike the front until the very last moment.

It all boils down to the jockey's fundamental dilemma: the horse is bred, primed and trained to run as fast as it can, but speed alone does not win races. That speed, and the animal's massive strength, have to be conserved and channelled. If on a front-runner, the jockey will need to be able to judge the pace exactly: is it so fast that the horse will not last home, or is it so slow that he will be caught from behind by a horse with 'a turn of foot' (the ability to accelerate)? On a horse which needs holding up, the rider has to judge how the other horses in the race are going and plot his move accordingly – then neither leave his mount too much to do to get to the front, nor get to the front too soon and risk the horse's thinking he has done enough and so easing off. (Despite those 55 million years of evolution, a horse is unlikely to understand the significance of that white pole with a red circle on top.)

For a jump jockey this fine judgement is complicated by the necessity of jumping obstacles at speed. If you are going to the last fence in second position, with a 'double handful' (alternatively, 'still plenty of horse under me'), you have to take into account how your partner might jump that fence. If you hold back and he jumps badly, your momentum – and chance – may have gone. If he jumps well and the other horse jumps badly, you may end up in front too soon. Decisions, decisions.

A different dilemma faces the jump jockey coming to the last fence well clear of the field. One fence to go, and if we jump it we win. One of the basic skills of the jump jockey is to tell the horse when to jump, but coming to the last ten lengths clear, do you play safe, allow the horse to go short and pop over, or do you take the positive route and, despite his (and your) tiredness, ask him to go long? There is not necessarily a right and a wrong way to resolve this conundrum, but get it wrong in the event and there will be no shortage of observers – the 'riders in the stand' – ready and willing to point out, often vociferously as you wipe the mud off your breeches and make the long walk back to the weighing room, exactly what you should have done.

That nerve-wracking moment of coming to the last well clear sharpens the focus on one of the most important skills a jump jockey needs, namely the ability when approaching a fence to 'see a stride' and present your horse at the obstacle in such a way that he will jump it with maximum fluency. Some horses are naturally flamboyant jumpers, launching themselves at each fence with gay abandon, and the sight of one of this select band – Tingle Creek, Desert Orchid, Dublin Flyer – in full flight provides racing with one of its most glorious spectacles. But even the best horses need to be guided, to be steered, and the worst horses need to be given a considerable amount of help – not always received in the spirit in which it is given.

But for all that it is important to get the horse jumping fluently, the greatest gift a jockey – like any equestrian sportsperson – can possess is 'a good pair of hands', the ability to have just the right contact with the horse's mouth through the reins. Be hard on a horse's mouth and he'll resent the discomfort and do nothing for you. Some horses have especially sensitive or 'light' mouths, and as soon as you get on one of these you can tell that he won't be messed about. Some you can play around with more. Some will settle in a race if you drop your hands early on and leave their mouths alone, while others will refuse to settle at any stage and will burn themselves out. The horse who pulls for his head throughout the early part of a race and fights his jockey's attempts to steady him is wasting too much energy, so the ability to get him to settle is vital.

In November I was riding That Old Feeling at Warwick for John White. He said the horse was 'a bit keen' – often a polite way of saying 'virtually uncontrollable' – and that Adrian Maguire had got run away with going down to the start on him last time out. So I tried to take him down very steady. At first he just trotted, then broke into a slow canter. That slow canter just got a bit quicker, then a bit quicker still. That Old Feeling was one of those horses who when you touch his mouth he'll piss off with you. So you try to go steady, steady, steady, but this horse ended up going a flat out gallop – not for very long, but it wound him up, and he finished nowhere. John White wasn't very impressed. Another bollocking.

With a horse like that it can be very difficult to avoid serious contact with the mouth. You put your finger in the neckstrap and try to switch him off – as I thought I had done – but he just got into a little canter and got quicker and quicker.

The more you know about each individual horse the better you will be able to ride it.

An example. In September 1996 I went to Bangor-on-Dee to ride Wakt. John White said pop out and make the running. I duly popped out and made it, but all the way we were being taken on by Tony McCoy on Warner's Sports. Tony had won on my horse last time out, and he knew perfectly well that she'd run a bit free and would not settle if another horse was in close attendance. Every time I hit the front Tony would take me on; every time I pulled back to go in behind him he'd drop back. As a consequence Wakt refused to calm down into a rhythm: she'd settle in front, and she'd settle in behind, but wouldn't settle upsides. It was a three-mile race, and after we'd gone a mile and a half she started to drop back.

I knew that she'd stay the trip and was probably just giving herself a breather, but instead of sitting still for a little while and letting her get her breath I started to get after her, and this unsettled her. At the twelfth fence I tried to get her to go long, but she put down and unseated me.

I'd learned my lesson, and next time I rode her, in a three-mile chase at Uttoxeter, I made no attempt to make the running but let her settle in third or fourth.

*After about a mile and a half she moved up to join the
leaders and really started racing when I wanted her to.
She finished second. It just goes to show how much
I'd learned from the Bangor race.*

To win just once. Any young jockey who took the title of
this book too literally as an aspiration would have limited
horizons.

But by the beginning of October 1996 Guy Lewis had not
even had one winner that season. Already the comparison
with the previous year was depressing. By the start of
October 1995 he'd had twenty-eight rides and two winners;
by the start of this October, twenty-seven rides but no
winners.

His twenty-eighth ride was Captain Khedive in the Burley
Fuel Effect Conditional Handicap Chase at Market Rasen on
Thursday 3 October, the first time that season he was aboard
an odds-on favourite: Captain Khedive, trained by Paul
Nicholls, started at the prohibitive price of 5–2 on to beat
just three opponents, and on form looked a certainty.

*Captain Khedive had top weight but was a worthy
odds-on chance, as his recent form was very decent,
and in the event he turned out to be a steering job.
My gran could have won on him.*

*Tony McCoy, who rode regularly for Paul Nicholls,
had ridden Captain Khedive last time out, and when I
asked him about the horse he told me that he could be
a bit of a dicey jumper. But at the first he picked up
before the wings of the fence, which rather caught me*

by surprise, and after that I kicked him into every fence, getting him to take off when I wanted to rather than when he wanted to. He jumped like a stag, took up the running three out, and won on the bridle. When I watched the video of the race later – always good for cheering yourself up when you're back on a losing streak – I was amused to hear racecourse commentator Mike Cattermole's comment as we approached the winning post: 'Guy Lewis hardly has to move a muscle, apart from his neck muscles as he checks over his shoulder.'

It was a facile success, but came as a huge relief – the first winner in a season which was already turning rather flat. But now I was off the mark. Though I'm not particularly superstitious I'm aware – as is any jockey – that your luck turns one way or the other, and to have ridden a winner at last was certainly a change of luck. There were plenty of jockeys who hadn't had a winner at all by then.

But there was a sting in the tail of that race, the sort of situation which the nobody jockey is always coming up against.

Captain Khedive was entered to run again three days after the Market Rasen race, in a quite valuable chase at Kempton Park – not one of Kempton's biggest days, but a cut above the sort of fixture I usually ride at. The horse's owners wanted me to ride again, but Paul Nicholls insisted that the more experienced jockey Philip Hide had the ride. I'd just won on the horse and already I'd been jocked off! I wasn't pleased as Captain

Khedive took a bit of knowing, and I felt that I'd got the best out of him at Market Rasen. But Paul Nicholls was adamant that Philip Hide should ride and that's what happened. On form they should have won and Captain Khedive started joint favourite, but fell when still holding every chance going down the back straight. I couldn't suppress the feeling that had I been on him he might have won.

Still, I'd won on him at Market Rasen. I was off the mark.

4

Jammed in Second Gear

*'They'd be putting a little black mark
by my name'*

DESPITE FRUSTRATIONS ON THE HOME FRONT, October brought Guy a second trip to the Czech Republic, and an experience shared by very few British jockeys: the chance to ride in the Velka Pardubicka.

Run over four and a quarter miles around a highly complex twisting and turning course which includes stretches across plough, the Velka Pardubicka is the Czech equivalent of the Grand National. English connections with the race go back to its first running, in 1874, which went to an English jockey named Sayers, riding Frantome; the first English-ridden winner in the modern era was Stephens Society, ridden by the amateur Chris Collins in 1973. English trainer Charlie Mann rode It's A Snip to victory in the 1995 race, and the success of the jockeys' visit to the Czech Gold Cup in June 1996 led to a repeat invitation for the Velka Pardubicka itself. This time Guy was joined by Richard Dunwoody, Norman Williamson and Ken Whelan.

Varadero, whom I'd ridden on my previous visit in June, did not after all run in the big race, so my Czech friend Tommy Jansa had said he'd see if he could find me a ride. There turned out to be a couple of spares – Cipisek and Double Odds. I was originally going to ride Cipisek, but the proposed rider of Double Odds, Vladislav Snitkovskij, had some disagreement with the owner: he took the ride on Cipisek and I got on to the other one.

This was the Czech version of Grand National day, and there was a wonderful atmosphere. I walked the course about six times to make sure I had it right: four and a quarter miles across country, some of it plough; twists and turns, some sharp, some not so sharp. The fences – thirty-two of them – make it look rather like a cross-country course in a three-day event, or a team chase. There's a stone wall, a six-foot upright bank, open water – and then there's the Taxis.

Some people say that the Taxis – the famous fence jumped only in the Velka Pardubicka itself – is a sort of Czech version of Becher's Brook, but Becher's is a very different proposition from this monster. From the take-off side the fence looks inoffensive enough – the sort of stiff hedge you'd think nothing of on a day's hunting. It's on the landing side that the full horror hits you: an enormous ditch with a long sloping lip out of it. Your horse wouldn't know about this until he was clearing the hedge, so you'd have to ride like the clappers into the fence and pray that you had enough momentum to clear the ditch.

I had a good long look at every fence, but the Taxis was the one which demanded real respect.

There was a crowd of forty thousand, a real buzz, and a huge amount of attention – and goodwill – directed at us visiting jockeys. Richard Davis had made a deep impression on our earlier visit, and to honour his memory the course staged the Richard Davis Memorial Chase, the race before the big one. I had a ride in this on Lateran, the horse Richard himself had partnered in the Czech Gold Cup, and we finished fourth: Richard's brother Stephen was there to present the prize.

The Velka Pardubicka, the final event of a nine-race programme, had twenty-one runners – a big enough field for all those twists and turns – with Richard Dunwoody riding the previous year's winner It's A Snip and Norman Williamson on Irish Stamp, trained by Ferdy Murphy.

My mount, the grey Double Odds, had won a few races but he was tiny, a little rat of a thing: I thought the size of some of the jumps would simply be too much for him – and sure enough, after all that preparation studying the fences, I didn't get very far.

All went well enough over the first three. The first two hedges are quite big, but Double Odds pinged those and my optimism started to rise. He pinged the third, too – the water – and then we turned the right-handed bend and started motoring as fast as we could towards the Taxis, trying to get up as much speed as possible to get to the other side and clear the lip of that *ditch. The closer we got to it, the more the hedge itself seemed to dwarf Double Odds, but there was no turning back. As we reached it he had a good look, backed off a little, then head-butted the fence, crashing through. On the other side he slammed into the lip of the ditch and buckled over. And that was that.*

Fell fourth: so much for all my preparation.

Double Odds galloped off, leaving me on the grass – a little cramp in my leg, but otherwise none the worse. As I sat on the floor, Dave Dent, who'd just taken a photo of my fall, came over with a cigarette and a drink for me! Then a Czech television crew started interviewing me – the race was still going on out in the country somewhere – and asking me what had happened. Answer: the horse fell. Simple as that.

Back home, that first win on Captain Khedive had not opened the flood gates, and the three weeks after Guy's return from the Czech Republic delivered a depressingly familiar sequence of races in which his mounts finished out with the washing – that is, if they finished at all.

Dai Burchell phoned me up and asked whether I'd ride Terrano Star in a novice chase at Ludlow. I knew that Dai junior – who often rode the horses his father trained – was not keen on the ride because of Terrano Star's reputation: Dai had been run away with by the horse in a bumper at Worcester.

Terrano Star had never run over fences before – though he had been point-to-pointing (and had fallen)

– and when I got to the races at Ludlow I confessed to Dai (junior): 'I shouldn't be doing this, should I?'

Dai didn't exactly boost my confidence: 'No – you're mad!'

The closer I got to the race, the more I was shitting myself. This horse was impossible to hold, and once he got to a fence was certain to fall. Mad, or what?

But if he was going to fall at least I could get off sharpish, so in the parade ring I pulled my irons up a couple of holes to ease a quick exit from the saddle when the inevitable moment came.

Once the race got under way, I managed to put Terrano Star in behind a couple of horses, and to my surprise he settled quite nicely. To my even greater surprise, he jumped the first well enough. The fences down the back straight at Ludlow come quickly, but the horse had found a nice rhythm, and I was hastily revising my opinion of him. A couple of the other runners fell, and with a circuit to go I was travelling sweet as a nut. I started to get a little cocky, gave him a squeeze going into a fence, asked him to go a little long – and he put down, clambered over, scraped his head along the floor, and I stepped off.

In the end I'd been right. I'd thought he'd fall and he did fall, but it was as much my mistake as his. Nine times out of ten, when beforehand you think, 'What on earth am I doing riding this?', it ends up quite all right.

Having pottered around quietly while the blue-bloods of the Flat hog the headlines in September and October with

their St Leger and their Prix de l'Arc de Triomphe and their
Breeders' Cup, the jumping season quickens its pace percep-
tibly from the middle of November.

The sequence of the season's big races begins with the
Murphy's Gold Cup (until the 1996–7 season the Mackeson
Gold Cup) at the mid-November Cheltenham meeting which
marks the arrival of the jumping game on centre stage. Big
races attract the top horses, and the seasonal reappearance of
favourite chasers and hurdlers gives this period of the racing
year a special mood.

On Mackeson day – sorry, Murphy's Gold Cup day – Guy
rode not at Cheltenham, where Richard Dunwoody was
giving an exquisite exhibition of the jump jockey's artistry
when winning the big race on Challenger Du Luc, but at the
much more lowly venue of Windsor. Braydon Forest started
third favourite in his race but was pulled up when tailed off,
and his second ride, Will James, finished seventh of eight.
Still, that was a couple of riding fees earned.

At the end of November came the Hennessy Cognac Gold
Cup at Newbury, after the Murphy's the second of the big
steeplechases of the season. Guy did not have a ride in the
Hennessy – indeed, he had never ridden in the race – but he
had reason to remember that Newbury meeting.

*On the Friday, the day before the Hennessy, I was
riding a horse named Honey Mount for Nick Walker.
Honey Mount was quite well fancied – 4–1 second
favourite in the market behind a David Nicholson
horse – and we fancied our chances a great deal:
he'd been working very well.*

The race was over two miles five furlongs – perhaps a little short of his best trip – and turning into the home straight he was absolutely cruising. Nick had told me to take it up turning in as the horse would just keep galloping, and might be a little one-paced.

Early in the straight I still had a double handful, and was sure he would win, so well was he travelling. The ground was a little bit dead on the inside so I went up the middle of the track, pulling towards the stand rail. But three flights out I hadn't worn the others off, and I felt Honey Mount stopping underneath me. Between the third last and the second last I thought perhaps the horse was having me on and gave him two or three quick cracks with the whip, then one more jumping the second last. I wouldn't normally hit a horse while jumping, but we were still upsides and still in with a chance. It was all to no avail, and we weakened to finish fifth.

Back in the weighing room I started changing out of my colours – no other rides that afternoon – when the stewards' secretary Paul Barton came in and said that the stewards wanted to see me.

'What about?'

'Your use of the whip.'

The whip has been a contentious issue in racing for many years.

For any rider, the whip is an essential tool for keeping a horse's mind on the business in hand, which for a jockey means getting your partner to run as fast as he can when you want him to, even when his instincts and his aching muscles are telling him to slow down. Additionally, the whip may be administered in the early stages of a race as a 'reminder' to the horse to concentrate, and waved alongside the horse in a finish as encouragement (or veiled threat) without contact being made at all.

But contact is the problem, and over the years racing authorities have become ever more aware of the public distaste for the sight of a horse apparently running his heart out and yet being belaboured with the stick.

According to current Jockey Club rules, the whip should be used 'for safety, correction and encouragement only', and not at all under certain circumstances (such as when a horse is clearly winning, or clearly out of contention), in certain ways (such as with the whip arm above shoulder height) and on certain parts of the horse.

With its roots in the uncompromising world of hunting, where men are men and horses are horses, jump racing has tended to stop short of sentimentality about the use of the whip, but matters came to a head at the National Hunt Festival meeting at Cheltenham in 1980. Irish jockey Tommy Ryan was handed a three-month ban from riding for what was deemed to be excessive use of the whip on two winners at the meeting, Mountrivers and Drumlargan. In the case of Drumlargan, the jockey candidly explained that 'with the money our lads had on this one I should have been lynched if we'd got beat'. But Ryan's compatriot Joe Byrne did indeed get beat – albeit very narrowly – in the Daily Express Triumph Hurdle after belting the living daylights out of his mount Batista, and informed opinion was adamant that the horse would have won had his jockey held him together rather than flogging him up the Cheltenham hill in heavy ground. Byrne received a similar punishment to Ryan.

The bans meted out to Ryan and Byrne came at a period when the Jockey Club was becomingly increasingly concerned about the damage that excessive use of the whip was doing to the public image of racing: two months before that Cheltenham meeting an instruction had gone out to local stewards to step up their scrutiny of whip use.

Official guidelines supporting that scrutiny later became more formal, including the stipulation that stewards should consider holding an inquiry whenever a horse was seen to be hit more than a specified number of times. The Rules then amended this provision, recasting it in more general terms: horses should not be hit with 'excessive frequency', and the stewards should take into account relevant factors such as the horse's experience, whether the horse was responding, and the degree of force used.

Interpretation of those guidelines can be fairly straightforward in some cases (thwack your horse on his head and it will be clear that you have done so), but is less clear-cut in others, and differing interpretations by different sets of stewards of what constitutes overstepping the mark is a recurrent cause of frustration to jockeys. The afterglow of many famous races has been dulled by controversy over the use of the whip. After Barnbrook Again and Waterloo Boy fought out their famous duel in the Queen Mother Champion Chase at Cheltenham in 1992, both jockeys – Hywel Davies and Richard Dunwoody – received bans for excessive use. The same occurred to Adrian Maguire and Declan Murphy after the great battle between Barton Bank and Bradbury Star for the 1993 King George VI Chase at Kempton Park. (Murphy subsequently appealed and became the first jockey to have a whip ban overturned. Maguire decided against an appeal.) Graham McCourt received a three-day ban after his sensational Cheltenham Gold Cup victory on 100–1 chance Norton's Coin in 1990, and two years later the same race saw the winning jockey stood down for four days: Adrian Maguire was adjudged to have hit his horse Cool Ground twenty times between the second last fence and the winning post: 'I was excessive,' he conceded, 'but you don't think of that during the Gold Cup and I wouldn't have won otherwise.'

'I wouldn't have won otherwise': there's the rub – and the nub of the problem. No jockey worth his salt is going to ease off if he thinks that a few more cracks with the whip are going to make the difference between victory and defeat. Be the race the Cheltenham Gold Cup or a selling hurdle at Bangor, it will not endear you to the trainer – or to many owners – if you slacken the pressure close home with the race there for the taking because you daren't incur the wrath of the stewards.

I knew I'd given Honey Mount two or three quick ones before the second last, but after that I hadn't hit the horse at all, so I couldn't understand what the problem was.

I duly padded off with Paul Barton to the stewards' room, where I stood outside like a naughty schoolboy awaiting the call into the headmaster's study. Then I was summoned in, to stand before the three stewards who were sitting behind their table. I tend to get a little angry when up before the stewards about whip use as I don't think I'm at all whip-happy. There's no point in giving a horse a little tap which he'll hardly feel. The horse is a big, thick-skinned animal, and when the adrenalin is flowing is unlikely to respond to a less than whole-hearted crack. The whip has to be used with discretion, and you can't tell how a horse is going to respond until you've had a go. When you've learned that response, the key is to use the whip in rhythm with the horse – to help him with it, not hinder him. So if you're in contention after the last, you'll give him one then let him run for a couple of strides before giving him the next one, then another one . . . couple of strides . . . another one . . . couple of strides. Watch Richard Dunwoody ride a finish and you'll see brilliant use of the whip: he might give the horse one, then, two or three strides later, another, then another if the horse is responding, then maybe switch the whip through to the other hand – all in the interests of helping the horse get home.

As you get to know individual horses, you learn how they will respond. My old favourite Channel Pastime, for instance, sticks his neck out and tries his best, so keeping after him with the whip isn't going to make any difference. If he's neck and neck upsides another horse at the last he'd tend to get beaten as he wouldn't have the turn of foot, and no amount of going at him with the whip is going to give it to him.

I've had two whip bans in my career. The first was when I won an amateur chase at Cheltenham in October 1993 on Mayoran. I was only eighteen, and the horse didn't help me at all. He was off the bridle all the way, and every time I gave him a backhander he'd pick up: I had to give him one every couple of fences, just to wake him up. After the third last he'd dropped right back, but he responded to the whip and picked up again. After the last he was third. I half thought I was beat, but I gave him another one and he picked up again, so I gave him another one. We made up ground on the leaders all the way up the run-in and I didn't put my stick down – gave him one, gave him one, gave him one – and we got up and won by a length. Everybody was saying what a great ride I'd given the horse but I knew I'd overstepped the mark with the whip, and wasn't surprised when I got four days' suspension. (When you're suspended you're barred from entering the weighing room area, including the changing room.)

My second ban came after a race at Exeter in October 1995. That time I was beaten half a length after a driving finish, and I'd given Herbert Buchanan six strokes after the last – the minimum at which the stewards had to consider your case. But that time they did me for force, not for frequency, and I was a bit miffed. The horse had not been marked: how could they tell how hard I was hitting him?

In the case of Honey Mount at Newbury I didn't think I'd transgressed significantly, so I was puzzled to be standing before the stewards.

The senior steward of the day told me that they were looking into my use of the whip on Honey Mount between the third last and second last hurdles. Then they showed me film of the race from all sorts of different angles – head-on, side-on, from behind – and invited my comments about why I'd hit the horse at various moments. I described how I thought Honey Mount was idling with me in front as we came to the second last, how I had to give him two or three sharp ones to wake his ideas up as I knew he was capable of winning a race like this. But I pointed out that as soon as I'd realised we were beaten, I'd been quite easy on the horse.

Indignant as I sometimes feel when brought before the stewards, it's important not to waffle on too much, as if you go over the top in your defence it doesn't always go down too well!

When they'd heard my evidence they asked me to wait outside, then after two or three minutes I was called back into the room for their verdict: no suspension this time, but they'd be putting a little black mark by my name and would be keeping an eye on me in the future.

On the whole, racecourse stewards are friendly and constructive towards jockeys, but the lack of consistency between stewards at one course and another is a constant bugbear. Use the whip in a certain way at one course and no one says anything. Use it in an identical way at another course the following day and you get a four-day suspension. That's crazy.

As it turned out, escaping a suspension following his ride on Honey Mount didn't make much difference to the amount of action Guy saw for the rest of the year. The whole of December yielded just ten rides.

Without enough rides no jockey can make a living, and for the journeyman a steady supply of rides is as essential as customers for a plumber or clients for a solicitor – and not simply because the £84.80 a time keeps the bank manager at bay. They are the lifeblood of a career that needs constant infusions if it is to survive, let alone develop – opportunities to display your skills and thus attract the attention of owners and trainers who will provide other rides, and opportunities occasionally to boot home winners.

But there are only a limited number of rides to go round, and the supply can be affected by all sorts of factors. A spell of wintry weather may mean frozen or waterlogged racecourses and abandoned meetings – and thus no rides for anyone. A spell of hot weather will harden the ground and make it difficult to train jumping horses to the level of fitness at which they can run, and risky to run them on some courses even if they are fit enough – which again means fewer rides up for grabs, and fewer still on decent horses.

Naturally enough, the leading riders can get more rides than their fellows at the foot of the jockeys' table. By Christmas 1996 Tony McCoy had partnered horses in no fewer than 415 races that season. His then closest pursuer for the jockeys' championship, Adrian Maguire, had recorded a considerably lower total: 279. Richard Dunwoody, in third place, had had 263. But Guy Lewis had ridden in just 63 races.

Arrangements regarding who rides a horse in a race have become much more fluid over recent years. Time was when the leading stables would each retain a top jockey who, in return for an annual payment, would be contractually bound to give rides for that stable preference over offers from any other source. In the late 1980s the Flat saw the emergence of a trend for top jockeys to be retained not by a trainer but by one of the mega-owners: first claim on the considerable talents of Willie Carson was bought by Sheikh Hamdan Al Maktoum for the last few years of his career, while Pat Eddery spent several seasons as first jockey to Khalid Abdullah. Jump racing does not have owners on the same scale as those who preside over the great empires on the Flat, but even so some of the biggest will have their own arrangements with particular jockeys: Paul Carberry, for example, rode for major owner Robert Ogden during the 1996–7 season. And sometimes an arrangement might be made whereby a top jockey commits himself to riding a top horse, even if that horse is not trained by one of his most regular employers: Richard Dunwoody and One Man come to mind.

Such arrangements at the elite end of the racing scale are unlikely to cause the journeyman jump jockey to lose much sleep: he is too busy garnering every ride available to worry about whether an agreement to ride a potential Gold Cup winner might get in the way of his agreement to ride whenever available for a top trainer. But two related – and comparatively recent – developments in the working patterns of jump jockeys do affect those at the humbler levels.

The first is that many of the top riders are avoiding commitments which would tie them to one particular trainer, preferring the freedom of the freelance existence. This means that while they may still have informal – or non-contractual – agreements to ride for a particular trainer when they are available, they would not be bound by such a tie should a better offer come up. It also means that the top jockeys are more often available to pick up 'spare' rides which otherwise might be fodder for the journeymen.

The other development is the rapid rise in the use of jockeys' agents, whose role is to represent to trainers the skills and availability of the jockeys on their books, in return for a percentage of the riding fee. (Valet, agent – those percentages do add up.) Say a top jockey is riding at one of the smaller tracks and has three rides on a six-race card for the stable for which he most regularly rides. His agent will study the entries for that meeting (when they are published, five days before the event) and assess likely spare rides for his client – then speedily phone the trainers of those horses and offer his jockey's services.

With such energy going into the mopping up of spare rides for the very top jockeys, the chances of the lesser-known pilot picking up such rides are diminished. And if you are a journeyman jockey and your agent happens to have more senior riders on his books, he is likely to offer their services before he offers yours. Which said, it is not all gloom for those at the wrong end of the pecking order. Different sorts of jockeys are required for different sorts of races and different sorts of horses. A trainer might need a rider for a conditional jockeys' race, for which no one with a full licence would be eligible; or he might be looking for someone to ride a horse at a weight that a more glamorous jockey could not manage.

Nowadays getting rides is so dominated by agents that trainers are not committing themselves to a jockey until the day before a race – when under the rules they have to declare who is going to ride their horses. If there's a trainer you ride for regularly, or a horse you've ridden before and you know to be your ride (such as Channel Pastime in my case), that's one thing. But without that sort of expectation, you're scrabbling around for rides.

I do have an agent, but he's mainly there to get me spares, and I do as much as I can to arrange my own rides.

You might be told four or five days in advance that you can ride a horse. Or you might be offered the ride out of the blue, late on; or you have to go looking. As soon as the declarations are made, five days before the meeting itself, I'll go through them in the racing press, marking off rides which I might be able to get, then phone the trainers and ask whether I can ride the horse. Sometimes I'm turned down flat, sometimes I'm offered the ride there and then. Most often the trainer suggests I call back in a couple of days – which gives them time to offer the ride elsewhere should someone better phone up.

It can pay to be bold. In March 1993, when I was still an eighteen-year-old amateur, I noticed that Martin Pipe – a trainer most struggling jockeys would love to ride for, as he's such a source of potential rides and winners – had the mare Re-Release entered in the Fulke Walwyn Kim Muir Challenge Cup for amateur riders on the first day of the Cheltenham National Hunt Festival. So I phoned Martin Pipe and asked if I could ride her, and he said: 'You ride.' Simple as that. The instructions he gave me before I got the leg-up in the paddock were unusual – get her into as much trouble as you can, she loves being bustled about – but she ran a blinder to finish fourth after being interfered with when the other Pipe runner, Roc de Prince, unseated his rider six fences out.

On another occasion, before the overnight declaration of jockeys was mandatory, I was riding at Lingfield Park and was told by one of Martin Pipe's representatives that I could ride Errant Knight the next day at Chepstow – and that the horse would win; all I had to do was phone Mr Pipe in the morning to get my instructions. I duly phoned:

'I'm told I ride Errant Knight this afternoon.'

'No, you don't.'

End of conversation.

Any spare that's worth riding – that looks like it can win, or at least get placed – will attract the attentions of agents on behalf of the top jockeys. But sometimes a horse you ring up to ride is no good whatsoever, and you're still told that Dunwoody or McCoy is riding it, since they happen to be at that meeting and have no prior commitments for that race.

What chance have you got to get rides, let alone winners, under those circumstances? But there's nothing much you can do about it except take it on the chin, keep your head down, and work away until you're up there with the big boys and there are little guys moaning about you!

On 9 December a nine-man jury at the inquest into Richard Davis's fall at Southwell just over four months earlier recorded a verdict of accidental death.

On the same day the Jockey Club released its own report on the circumstances surrounding the jockey's death, raising questions about medical arrangements at the course but expressing itself satisfied that the track itself was in an entirely satisfactory condition, that Mr Sox was fit to run in the race, and that Laura's Shally's training facilities met the licensing requirements for a permit-holder.

In a supplementary report, a working group set up by the Jockey Club made various recommendations: that additional standards be set which a prospective trainer would have to meet before being granted a licence; that licensing criteria for conditional jockeys be tightened up (though this was not directly relevant to the Davis case); that the performances of horses be more closely monitored, with horses which seemed to be persistently bad jumpers being re-schooled and assessed (and banned for the rest of the season if failing again next time out); and that experiments be undertaken in the use of practice fences or hurdles which could be taken on the way to the start.

For Guy, the turn of the year was approaching, and his season was jammed in second gear. The frustrations of this period, as well as the dangers of riding racehorses and the sheer perseverance required of the journeyman professional jockey were all epitomised in one ride the week before Christmas. The horse was Cashel Quay, a 100–1 shot in a Bangor-on-Dee bumper: races don't come much humbler than that. As Guy mounted in the parade ring, Cashel Quay

– for no apparent reason – reared up and fell back down o
top of his jockey – who, with the fortitude expected of hi
trade, got up and tried again.

They finished – guess – tailed off.

Richard Davis 1969–1996.

Guy Lewis, boy, man . . . and woman.

First winner at Cheltenham, September 1993. Guy on Bankroll (right) and Peter Hobbs on Newton Point at the last hurdle: Bankroll won by a head.

First Grand National, March 1996. Guy at the nineteenth fence on Brackenfield: 'One! Two! Three! . . . But this time he said Four!, put his hind legs in the ditch and hit the fence as if it were a brick wall.'

Pardubice, the Czech Republic, October 1996.

Left: Guy getting the measure of the Taxis with fellow jockeys Richard Dunwoody, Norman Williamson and Ken Whelan.

Below: The Velka Pardubicka: Guy (black and white stripes) parts company with Double Odds at the Taxis.

All in a day's work.

Lining up.

Winners:
above, Night Boat at Bangor, 22 March 1997;
below, Chan The Man at Hereford, 26 May 1997.

5

The Freeze

'One slice of turkey and a very small portion of vegetables for Christmas dinner'

THE CHRISTMAS PERIOD IS A BUSY TIME FOR jockeys. Ten jumps meetings scheduled for Boxing Day (which in 1996 fell on a Thursday) and five the following day, with the weekend and New Year to follow on, seemed to offer plenty of opportunities for a few decent paydays.

Five Boxing Day rides booked at Market Rasen, in deepest Lincolnshire, not far from Grimsby and a hell of a trek from South Wales. But it looked worth it; I hadn't had as many as five rides on one card all season. One of these, Banntown Bill, was for Martin Pipe: my third ride for the stable, and not without a chance. A good run here could have led on to other rides for Martin Pipe, a tremendous step in the right direction.

But Banntown Bill was set to carry ten stone, which with my three-pound allowance meant I had to do nine eleven. One of my other rides was also on ten stone, and in any case putting up any overweight would not have greatly impressed Mr Pipe.

So it was a pretty abstemious Christmas Day. One slice of turkey and a very small portion of vegetables for Christmas dinner, and one glass of dry white wine. My usual sauna at the local hotel was not open on Christmas Day, so after lunch I took myself upstairs for a hot bath – the temperature as high as I could stand, and the hot water regularly topped up – to sweat off the effect of that binge. After an hour's sweating I was three pounds lighter.

The weather was deteriorating and the forecast was gloomy. Several of the Boxing Day fixtures had already been threatened, but Market Rasen looked likely to go ahead: they were expecting frost up there but had taken all sorts of precautions. Fingers crossed.

Another hot bath before going to bed to lose a couple more pounds, and for a nightcap a soft laxative to ensure that I'd be able to clear myself out in the morning.

Woke up Boxing Day about seven and weighed myself: nine eight. Perfect. No more weight to lose, so I'd be able to have a drink or a piece of fruit on my way up to Market Rasen (a drive of four hours plus), and if I needed to lose another pound I could sit in the sauna up there.

Checked Ceefax: the weather had taken a grip. No Market Rasen. No five riding fees. No chance to remind Martin Pipe of my skills.

So instead of setting off on that hopeful trek to

*Lincolnshire, I made my way to the meet of the local
hunt – to find that that had also been called off because
of the weather. My brother-in-law Nick had gone
along, and we adjourned to the nearest pub for the
afternoon. I got home pie-eyed about seven. There was
a party locally that evening, and I thought I'd have a
quick zizz before getting ready to go out . . .*

*. . . Woke up at four in the morning. I weighed
myself: nine stone five! I'd lost another three pounds
from the dehydration of drinking.*

Market Rasen was one of nine meetings abandoned on
Boxing Day 1996. The other eight were Ayr, Hereford,
Huntingdon, Newton Abbot, Sedgefield, Wetherby,
Wincanton and Wolverhampton (where jump racing was due
to be inaugurated on a new turf course alongside the recently
established all-weather track: in the event jumping did not
return to Wolverhampton until 11 May 1997.) The only
fixture which went ahead was the most prestigious, the
biggest day of the year at Kempton Park, where the King
George VI Chase was won in brilliant style by One Man,
ridden by Richard Dunwoody. It was Dunwoody's fourth win
in the race.

The cancellation of so many meetings on one of the sport's
major days was a grievous setback – albeit a not unfamiliar
one – for the racecourses themselves, for tens of thousands of
racegoers who traditionally flock to Boxing Day fixtures as a
way of countering Christmas Day excesses, and not least for
those participants for whom no sport meant no pay. No one
would be compensating Guy for loss of riding fees which

would have totalled over well over £400 even without the expectation of any percentages for winning or being placed.

Of the five meetings scheduled for the Friday, the day after Boxing Day, only Musselburgh, nestling in a particularly kindly climate on the coast near Edinburgh, survived. The Saturday was a wipe-out – no jump racing at all, just an all-weather fixture on the Flat at Wolverhampton to provide fodder for betting-shop punters – and the jumping world started to come to terms with the exasperating prospect of a prolonged spell without any racecourse action. Between Musselburgh on Friday 27 December and Carlisle and Leicester on Tuesday 14 January, only one of the thirty-eight scheduled National Hunt fixtures in Great Britain went ahead – and that one, again at Musselburgh on 10 January, was too remote from his usual stamping ground to be of much use to Guy Lewis, who eventually resumed race riding at Taunton on 16 January after a break of three and a half weeks.

Some of the top jockeys actually welcome an enforced break as it gives them a chance to recharge their batteries after the grind of five or six rides a day, six or seven days a week. I don't have that problem, and it's infuriating for racing to be wiped out by the weather. Nor was there much serious exercising of horses to be done. Many of the all-weather gallops were frozen, and in any case most of the trainers I ride out for are not well off enough to have all-weather gallops. The horses have to be kept on the move as much as possible, but this mostly means road work.

I didn't have much to do, and I found the break boring as well as exasperating. Just when things could have taken a real turn for the better, with a winner at Market Rasen on Boxing Day, perhaps the Martin Pipe horse, now here I was lounging round the house trying to find ways of keeping myself occupied. Without the incentive of race riding to make me keep an eye on my weight, I found myself eating and drinking more, and I started putting on the pounds.

Getting fatter was one problem. Getting unfitter was another. Many casual observers of racing don't appreciate just how fit you have be to ride racehorses, figuring that it's the horse who's putting in most of the athletic effort, and all the jockey has to do is sit there. The truth of the matter is very different, and jockeys have to be as fit as any sportsmen: indeed, someone who was researching these things figured out that riding in a race requires physical effort equivalent to running the 800 metres at top level – and often a jockey will be putting in that effort several times an afternoon, with only half-hour intervals in between.

The only proper way to keep in tune for race riding is to ride in races, so the longer the lay-off continued the more the key muscles started to sag. I kept in reasonably good shape by running, swimming and playing squash. (Later in the season Richard Davis's parents gave me his mechanical horse, a sort of carpet-clad de luxe rocking horse, complete with little ears, internally sprung to replicate – to a degree – the motion of a galloping horse. A few minutes on this each day, sometimes with weights on my hands, help keep the riding muscles in trim.)

Financially a long break with no racing is disastrous. Had I been sidelined through injury during that period I'd have had the Professional Riders' Insurance Scheme paying me money: an injured jockey receives a weekly sum calculated according to how many rides he gets, and that sum is paid whether racing is going ahead or not. But as it is I had no income whatsoever.

The freeze-up didn't do the horses any good, either. They dislike the cold, and most of all they dislike inactivity. Road work isn't enough to keep them fully fit, and so once the weather relented and they were able to get back on to the racecourse most of them were in need of the run as they'd been short of real work for so long.

I had two rides on my first day back at Taunton. The first was Eleanora Muse, who never got into contention. The other was Sober Island, a 66–1 chance in a quite well-contested novices' handicap hurdle. It hadn't proved easy to remove the effects of all that food and drink during the layoff, and I had to put up two pounds overweight. Not that the excess made much difference to Sober Island, who got tailed off and passed the post last of the finishers.

Out with the washing as usual, but it was a relief to be back in action.

My next ride, two days later, was at a course rather further afield than Taunton: Catterick in North Yorkshire, where I'd been booked to ride Curragh Peter in the novice chase. He had no serious chance, but a ride is a ride. On the other hand, Catterick is Catterick, from South Wales a round trip of God knows how many hundred miles.

Brian Clifford and Timmy Murphy had also been booked for this tour of the frozen north, and early that morning I drove over to Warwick to meet up with them. As we set off on the long drive northwards we started talking about whether any of us was in his right mind – each flogging up there for just one ride, each on a no-hoper in an eighteen-runner novice chase. What was the point? We toyed with the idea of ringing through to the trainers and saying our car had broken down and we wouldn't be able to get there, and then repairing to the nearest pub. But we pushed such an unprofessional notion to one side, and continued on our way up north.

Curragh Peter started at 50–1, the same price as Timmy Murphy's horse. Brian's was even less fancied: 200–1. A two-mile eighteen-runner novice chase at Catterick turned out to be a pretty hairy experience. We went to the first fence like shit off a shovel, and I was flat to the boards straight away. Brian's 200–1 shot lived up to his billing by running out at the first (I think Brian was quite relieved!), but Timmy's and mine got round – in their own time.

Then that drive home.

All in a day's work.

It may have been a day's work, but in terms of payment that trio of jockeys would hardly have been worse off had they given in to temptation, played truant and let someone else take the risks that afternoon.

In January 1997 the basic riding fee per ride under National Hunt Rules (steeplechase, hurdle or 'bumper') was £84.80, raised from £80 the previous summer. (The sum is inclusive of VAT for a conditional jockey, exclusive of VAT for a fully fledged jockey.)

From that £84.80 are made various deductions: 10 per cent to your valet; 10 per cent to your agent (and in plenty of cases agents expect a cut even if the ride has not been booked by them); 50p (in the case of a conditional jockey) to the British Horseracing Board for industry training. And against what remains after those deductions must be set the considerable expenses which a jump jockey faces. At the head of the list for most would be the cost of travel. A professional jockey will drive at least 50,000 miles a year, and although those at the top of the tree may be able to flit from meeting to meeting by hiring a light aeroplane or helicopter (and thereby increase their number of rides, as this way they can easily ride at two meetings in a day), that is a luxury which few of the journeymen ever enjoy. Instead they rush around the country in cars, clocking up the mileage and piling up the petrol receipts, sharing with their comrades when they can to spread the load.

Sweet wrappers, cigarette packets, newspapers and all sorts of other detritus of his working life give Guy Lewis's car a distinctly lived-in look – testimony to the amount of time he spends in it flogging around to Taunton and to Bangor and to Stratford and to Towcester and to Warwick to pick up that lift to Catterick. Petrol is a major running cost; keeping the car on the road is another. Like most jockeys' cars, Guy's is sponsored – in his case this season by Channel Pastime's owners Mel and Sandra Worthington, who pay for the insurance in return for having the names of their respective businesses painted on the sides of the car, proclaiming their support of 'GUY LEWIS – NATIONAL HUNT CONDITIONAL JOCKEY'. By the standards of most professional sportsmen, it is a meagre level of sponsorship. Success breeds success which breeds attention and fame which breed more sponsorship, and until you reach the higher levels you have to get it where you can. In any case, jump jockeys suffer from a low level of public recognition – possibly because when they are most visible, that is when they are actually racing, their heads are all but enclosed in crash helmets, often with a layer of mud to obscure the bits that are exposed – and lucrative sponsorship and anonymity do not mix too well.

Another constant drain on resources is the necessity to have adequate equipment. A decent racing saddle can cost up to £300; a new pair of boots £150; a new skull cap £40. These are the tools of the trade, and like all good tools they don't come cheap; and the job can't be done without them.

The journeyman jump jockey does not have many potential sources of additional income. Not for him the guest appearance on *The Morning Line*, the invitation to open the local betting shop, or the brown envelope for going through the day's racing prospects for a group of guests in a racecourse hospitality suite. Nor do activities more directly related to his trade pay particularly well – or, indeed, at all. If he rides out or goes to school a few horses for a trainer, he will be doing so not for payment (probably none will be offered) but for the chance of getting rides from that stable.

There is, of course, one obvious source of supplementary income – his slice of the winnings.

The share of the prize money which the jockey receives for riding the winner of a race, or one of the other placed horses, is determined by an arcane formula laid down in the Jockey Club Rules and depends on the nature of the race. For example, the race which Guy won on Captain Khedive at Market Rasen came into the category where the winning jockey would receive 5.93 per cent of the total prize money – that is, of the prize money to be distributed among the connections of all placed horses. So in addition to his riding fee of £84.80, Guy would have received the sum of £307.17.

It is here at the sharp end, in the distribution of purses, that the disproportion in prize money between jump racing and the Flat becomes particularly painfully apparent. A Flat jockey in January 1997 was on a fee per ride of £61.50 as opposed to the £84.80 which his jumping comrade earned, but prize money on the Flat is very much larger than over jumps: the total annual pool is distributed in an approximate ratio of 60:40 in aid of racing on the level. So in 1997 total prize money for the most prestigious race on the Flat, the Derby, was, in round numbers, £1 million; for the most prestigious race over jumps, the Cheltenham Gold Cup, roughly a quarter of that. There are explanations for this disproportion (the need for the Flat to compete with other major racing nations, etc.), but the fact is that lower levels of prize money for the jumping fraternity mean lower payments to the participants. It is the top Flat riders, with their shares of huge purses and their nominations to the stallions whose reputations they have helped make on the racecourse, who become the millionaires of the jockeys' world.

The labyrinthine calculations officially laid down in the rules stipulating how prize money is to be shared out do not tell quite the whole story. Alongside that strictly defined system exists a black (or at least a grey) economy of racing in which custom dictates that the owner of a winner gives an additional 'present' to the winning rider – usually 10 per cent of the prize money won. (You will sometimes hear a race commentator suggesting that a jockey winning very easily has time to be 'working out his percentage'.)

That present will be donated directly. The rest of a jockey's earnings are paid through an account which each rider has at Weatherbys, the administrative arm of racing – popularly characterised as the sport's civil service – which is based in Wellingborough, Northamptonshire. Every month Guy receives from Weatherbys an account and a cheque. On the credit side, the account lists fees for his rides and any percentages for wins or places; on the debit side it lists deductions to his valet (fees to his agent he will pay direct). The Weatherbys account will also include any deductions for fines incurred – though this kind-hearted organisation allowed him to pay off the £250 fine from the weighing-in problem at Market Rasen in five monthly dollops of £50.

According to popular myth, a £250 setback is as nothing against the sort of sums a jockey might take in dropsy for riding in a race with, shall we say, less of a commitment to winning than might usually be expected. For some people outside racing, it is inexplicable that the owner or trainer of a horse in a race might not want it to win; yet there are many reasons why a horse might be given an easy race to the extent of avoiding victory. Most innocent of these is that he may not be fully fit, and may 'need the run' in order to get more tuned up; if he can win he will, but if during the course of the race that seems unlikely, he will not be put under too much pressure. More underhand is the stratagem of deliberately having a horse lose – 'stopping' him or 'hooking him up' with the full connivance of owner and trainer. Why on earth would they want him not to win? So that his handicap mark does not get too high and connections can plan to 'land a touch' – make a good deal from backing the horse – in a future race. This calculation has two elements: first, a horse that is not winning will be more leniently treated – given a lighter weight, that is – by the handicapper; and second, a few modest runs when 'not off' (not trying to win) will make a horse look more moderate than he is, and he will then start at longer odds when he *is* 'off'. Jockey Club Rules insist that a horse run on his merits in every race, and every yard of every race is closely studied by the stewards, through the medium of cameras sited around the course, in case a 'non-trier' should be up to these tricks.

The other person who might want a horse not to win is a crooked bookmaker. If there is a hot favourite in a race and a bookmaker knows for a fact that it will not win, he can make a killing by offering that horse at longer odds than his fellow bookies and thus attract a large amount of money, secure in the knowledge that he will not have to pay out. The betting ring is closely monitored and such shenanigans are rare, but they do happen; and the surest way to ensure that a horse is not going to win is to get at his jockey.

For Guy Lewis, such matters are of academic interest.

I've only ridden three or four dead certainties in my whole career, and none of them attracted the attention of a bent bookie!

The only time I've ever been asked by an owner not to win was on a horse who was a complete outsider and had no possible chance whatsoever. We pulled up.

Occasionally an owner will quietly tell me in the paddock, 'I fancy this,' but that makes no difference to me. I can only do my best in every race, and if the horse can win, I want it to do so as much as the owner does.

Jockeys are expressly forbidden from betting, on any race at all – never mind whether or not you're riding in it – but there are ways of backing a horse which don't necessarily involve going round the betting ring in your riding silks with a wad of fivers in your hand. A jockey might tip off a connection who will back the horse and give the jockey a present for the information if the horse wins. The rules try to cover all these variations, but it does go on, and it's an open secret in the weighing room that some jockeys have close associations with big punters.

The racing programme had falteringly got back into its stride by the time 1997 was a couple of weeks old, but for Guy things were still moving ponderously, the returns on effort expended still low. January brought an extensive tour of the motorway system – to Taunton, Catterick, Wincanton, Folkestone, Doncaster, Warwick, Windsor, Towcester and

Taunton again – but only eleven rides. February was a little busier, but much quieter than he would have liked. No winners from eighteen rides – one of which got him into hot water with a fellow rider.

Jump jockeys may be noted for their camaraderie, but although they will chat to one another (even tell jokes) in the quieter stages of a race, once the tapes have gone up there is an unspoken etiquette of race riding which you breach at your peril. Among the worst crimes is trying to steal up the inside of a rival jockey (especially one senior to yourself), a manoeuvre which can result in dangerous scrimmaging – and fierce reactions from the affronted party. It can also result not only in opprobium when you get back to the weighing room, but in a distinct lack of sympathy from officialdom. When Peter Scudamore tried to block an attempt by Bruce Dowling to come up the inner approaching the cross hurdle at Newbury in 1988, the resulting argy-bargy left both jockeys with a three-week suspension. Adrian Maguire tried it on with Richard Dunwoody in a notorious incident at Nottingham in February 1994, at the height of their duel for the jockeys' championship: Dunwoody's move to shut out Maguire forced his rival's horse to run out, and Dunwoody was soon booking an unscheduled holiday.

Any wayward action which might seem to be endangering one of your fellow jockeys is met with a cool response; but hampering your senior colleagues is an occupational hazard for the journeyman.

I was riding Boozys Dream, 100–1 in a maiden hurdle at Wincanton – a very poor horse in a very poor race, though many of the top jockeys were riding. Boozys Dream had run twice in bumpers but had never raced over hurdles before, and as I'd not schooled him I wasn't sure how he'd jump.

He pulled very hard from the start, and didn't seem to have a clue what he was doing when he got to the first hurdle. He dived at it – never lifted a leg, just crashed through it. At the second hurdle he again walloped straight into it, landed sideways and took Norman Williamson's horse Fairy Knight, who was third favourite, sideways with me. I couldn't do much about it: it was the usual rough and tumble of an eighteen-runner maiden hurdle, and in those races you're lucky to get a proper look at the hurdle at all, let alone coax a beautifully executed jump out of your horse. Boozys Dream got tailed off and I pulled up before the third last.

When I got back to the weighing room Norman gave me a right bollocking: What did you think you were doing? You shouldn't have a licence, etc. I was livid. Norman's a top jockey riding class horses – practically everything he rides has a chance. I'm struggling to make a living riding bad horses, and I've got to ride whatever horse I can take: he never has to ride horses like that. Most times when a senior jockey has a go I'd just put my head down and say sorry, but this time I got angry. It blew over quickly enough, but the incident brought home how difficult it is when you're riding crap horses. I wish I didn't have to ride them, but I do.

Bad horses get in the way of good horses – it's a fact of racing life – and the jockeys on the better runners will try to avoid the worse ones. But that's easier said than done in an eighteen-runner field. The jockey on the bad horse can't just stay out of the way of the better, just stay at the back looking after yourself in deference to the better jockeys, as you've got to be seen to be giving your horse a decent ride, however outclassed you think he is. Otherwise the owner and trainer aren't going to be too happy with you. If you're in there among the other runners, giving your horse every possible chance, you're risking getting in the way.

You ride the bad horses because that trainer might have a good horse for you to ride in the future – and even if he doesn't, it's that fee in your pocket.

Sometimes, leaving aside the result of the race, you just can't win.

6

The Daily Grind

*'I wonder how far behind Tony McCoy
I am now . . .'*

NATIONAL HUNT RACING MAY BE KNOWN colloquially as the Winter Game, but the time when every season comes to a head, when earlier aspirations and expectations are resolved, when the plot of the year reaches its denouement, is the spring.

The Cheltenham National Hunt Festival in March and the Grand National meeting at Aintree a few weeks later form the twin peaks of jump racing's year, on which all owners, trainers and jockeys set their sights.

For most journeyman jockeys Cheltenham or Aintree glory is just an improbable dream, but even to ride at these famous meetings, to sample the buzz and be part of the action, is a target in itself. If you can't get in on the big-time action, there is still a living to be eked out around the gaffs, though with ground conditions beginning to get firmer as spring takes hold and fewer jump meetings taking place, finding rides can be even more of a struggle than usual. It's also time to start thinking about next season, to put in place arrangements which will mean a steadier supply of work, which in itself might lead you off the plateau towards the higher levels.

From early in March 1997 Guy Lewis kept a diary to chronicle the ups and downs of the journeyman's life at this crucial part of his season.

Monday 3 March
Windsor today for one ride: Achill Prince in a conditional jockeys' handicap hurdle. Ten stone. Monday isn't a great day to be doing ten stone, especially when you've been out partying on the weekend, but after a sweat in the course sauna I was all right. Achill Prince, a 33–1 shot, wore a muzzle and pulled like mad, but I got him round. Finished at the back, as expected.

Wednesday 5 March
A nightmare of a morning. Rode out two lots for Bill Clay. Left my car keys in the car and got locked out of it, so I ended up having to drive half an hour to Stafford in someone else's car to get a new key cut, then get back to the yard to collect my own and drive to Bangor. Supposed to have two rides, one a novice chaser, first time over fences, the other in the selling hurdle – but the hurdler didn't run and the chaser, Jasons Farm, didn't get very far. He'd jumped all right for the first mile, then got very tired on the soft ground and absolutely annihilated the open ditch, so I pulled up pretty quick. A bad day at the office.

Thursday 6 March
Another bad day. Rode out two lots for Bill Clay in the morning, then to Towcester: Becky's Girl in the novice chase for Roy Brotherton. Roy was on his own, so I had to saddle the mare up with him. I didn't like the look of her much: she was trying to do somersaults as we put her tack on, but she settled down a bit once we'd got to the start. Jumped the first three fences not too bad, then walked into the open ditch and fell. I got kicked around, and drove home feeling stiff and sore.

Friday 7 March
Got my monthly Weatherbys cheque – £1,500. But my petrol bill is £400 for the month, my agent's bill £250, phone bill £150 – doesn't leave me a lot.

Saturday 8 March
Sandown Park and Chepstow were the only fixtures today, and there was nothing for me to ride at either, so I went to a point-to-point instead. Spent the rest of the day sorting out my rides for Monday, the day before the Cheltenham Festival. Three meetings in the south and I've got possibilities at all of them, but I'll probably go to Stratford to ride Riverbank Rose for Bill Clay. I rode her the other day when she finished third at Doncaster – ran really well. But if I go to Stratford I'll be missing a couple of reasonable rides at Taunton. Knowing my luck at the moment I'll pick the wrong meeting.

Monday 10 March

Another winner! I decided after all to go to Stratford to ride Riverbank Rose, thus missing Chris's Glen in the first at Taunton. I thought that one would win, but for once I played things right. Chris's Glen was last of three finishers (thank God!), and Riverbank Rose made all and won by ten lengths. Everyone was extremely chuffed. My first winner for ages. I'd had seventy – seventy!! – rides since my last one, Captain Khedive at Market Rasen way back at the beginning of October, so this couldn't have come soon enough.

As Guy got into his car at Stratford that Monday evening to drive back to South Wales, not far away at Cheltenham racecourse the finishing touches were being made to preparations for the National Hunt Festival, the flagship event of the sport.

Here every March the very best horses come together to compete in twenty races. From the opening event, the Supreme Novices' Hurdle on the Tuesday, to the closing, the County Hurdle as night starts to fall on the Thursday, every one is fiercely contested, a major race in its category, with two in particular quickening the pulse of the massive crowds: the Champion Hurdle on the Tuesday and the Gold Cup (in spite of the Grand National's fame the most important steeplechase of the year) on the Thursday. On these, as on all races at the Festival, gargantuan amounts of money change hands in the maelstrom of the Cheltenham betting ring.

Guy Lewis has never ridden in the Champion Hurdle or Gold Cup, has never partnered a winner at the National

Hunt Festival. But he has sampled the meeting's unique atmosphere, having ridden at three Festivals before 1997, and was itching to repeat the experience, even if his conveyance was not a horse likely to be transporting him into the winner's enclosure.

Wednesday 12 March
The Cheltenham Festival.

Just the one ride this year, Prussia for Bill Clay in the Royal SunAlliance Hurdle, the opening race on the middle day. Prussia was really only here for the run round, as he had little realistic chance against the likes of the very good Irish novice Istabraq, and started at 200–1; he ran as well as I'd expected he would, and finished tailed off. That's about as good as he is in that sort of company. But the owner had a good day out and so did I. I suppose I could have had a couple of rides down at Newton Abbot, today's other meeting, but I always get a real buzz from being at the Festival. Fantastic mood in the weighing room – all the guys really geed up, and all those jockeys over from Ireland adding to the mood. Even when you're riding a no-hoper there's something very special indeed about this meeting. Out in the country it's just like riding in any race anywhere, but going past those huge jam-packed stands you can really taste the atmosphere: there's a tremendous roar from the crowd even when you pass first time round. After the race the finishers go back to the unsaddling area by walking all the way down past the stands, and the reception which the winner gets rubs

*off on you even if you've finished nowhere. My race was
duly won by Istabraq, owned by J. P. McManus and
ridden by Charlie Swan, and the noise pouring down
from the stands as we came back in after the race was
deafening: all Ireland must have been on him!*

Consider the reports of support for Istabraq in the betting
ring that day and you can understand the euphoria. Recorded
bets at odds of 11–8 included £27,500 to £20,000 three
times and £22,000 to £16,000 twice; in all he was backed to
take around £250,000 out of the ring and started at 6–5, the
biggest gamble of the meeting. What proportion of the
winnings went into the pocket of Istabraq's owner, the
legendary Irish punter J. P. McManus, is not known, but he
can be assumed to have taken home a satisfactory amount –
and if he did who could begrudge it him, after the battering
his fortunes had taken on the first day of the meeting?
Finnegan's Hollow, his runner in the first race, had fallen at
the third last hurdle when cruising into the lead, and later
that afternoon his chaser Time For A Run was beaten a neck.
You lose some, you win some.

As far as jockeys were concerned, the hero of the meeting
was Tony McCoy, who won the Champion Hurdle on Make
A Stand for Martin Pipe and two days later completed a rare
double when taking the Gold Cup on the giant white-faced
chestnut Mr Mulligan. McCoy was the second rider in three
years to land the Champion Hurdle–Gold Cup double,
following Norman Williamson in 1995, but before that you
have to go back to Fred Winter in 1961 for the equivalent
achievement.

As the Festival came to a close on the Thursday evening, Tony McCoy had plenty to celebrate, and his fellow jockeys would be on hand to help.

Friday 14 March
Woke up this morning with a bit of a head – and I won't have been the only one. After the Cheltenham Festival all the jockeys go out and have a few drinks, and at three o'clock this morning everyone – Tony included – was still going strong at a club in Cheltenham called Gas. No rides today, but a couple tomorrow at Hereford: I'll get my head fixed by then.

Saturday 15 March
The ups and downs of race riding. Two rides at Hereford: Kadari in a handicap hurdle, then Jasons Farm in the novice chase. I was very hopeful that Kadari would score as she'd finished third last time out at Southwell, and only one of her four rivals today had much form. She was hard work, though, and it took a lot out of me; she was never on the bridle, so I had to push and shove, push and shove, all the way – and it was a pretty hot day. She didn't help me at all in the race, but did manage to keep her nose in front after being headed and then regaining the lead two out, and won by a length and a half from the hot favourite Swing Quartet.

Two winners in a week! I'm running again, I'm flying . . . Then in the very next race I came down to earth with a very big bump.

After the effort of getting Kadari round I was feeling pretty lousy by the time I got the leg-up on Jasons Farm. At Bangor the previous week I'd pulled him up after about a mile because he wasn't going well on the soft ground; but he'd jumped fine. This time we got no further than the first fence. He met it spot-on, but just as he was about to take off the horse in front jumped to the left across us. Jasons Farm was distracted from the fence, never lifted a leg, landed on the top of his head and ploughed me into the ground. As he got up he kicked me in the eye.

I was lying on the floor, blood all over my face, my eye swelling up, and I couldn't see a thing. Completely dazed and beginning to get a bit worried, I got taken back to the weighing room in an official's car. Jasons Farm's trainer Bill Clay was waiting for me when I got there, but I couldn't see him until I got up really close: I told him I was OK, though I wasn't so sure. Back in the weighing room I had a lie down, and after a while my eyesight started coming back: all blurry and white at first, then images in black and white, then the colours started coming back. The course doctor came to check me out, but I assured him I was all right.

I couldn't have got on a horse again for a while, so it was lucky I didn't have any more rides that afternoon. Looked like I'd have to have a couple of days off.

That was my 101st ride of the season and my first serious fall, so I suppose I can't complain too much.

Sunday 16 March
Cuts and bruises all over.

Injury is something you never think much about when you're riding – in the sense that you don't find yourself wondering whether you're going to get hurt. You may have it in the back of your head, and before a race, if you're riding something you know to be a bad jumper, you'll be wondering what might happen, but once the race is under way you don't give it another thought. If it happens, it happens. You have three options at a fence: go long, go short or let him fiddle it: you just hope you choose the right one.

When it does happen it's usually so quick that your reactions are just instinctive: roll yourself into a ball and hope for the best. (If you have arms and legs sprawled out all over the place, you're more likely to have another horse tread on you.) So much depends on where you are in the field. The best place to be to keep out of trouble – to avoid horses trampling on you – is on the inner, so that if you should fall you can get out of the way pretty smartish under the rails. The same applies to the outside, but usually trainers are not keen for you to be keeping away from trouble on the outer. When you're in among the other runners, down the middle, is when you can really get kicked about. In any case, most falls look much worse than they feel to the jockey. Often a horse will clout the fence, lose his balance, hit the floor on the other side and just roll out the way, but particularly nasty is when your horse somersaults, its back end coming up

and landing straight on top of you. That's what
happened to Richard at Southwell.

    You tend to get the worst falls off the best horses.
With a bad horse you're half expecting it to fall and are
subconsciously bracing yourself, but with a good horse
it's more of a surprise, and everything seems to happen
so much more quickly. And falls over hurdles are much
worse than over fences, as the races are run at a faster
pace.

    When the average person sees a jockey fall and the
other horses going over him, they think we're
extremely courageous. Sometimes I see one myself and
think: Shit! – we must be brave! But I'd be more fright-
ened of a big spider or a snake than of a fall. I've been
very lucky in that I haven't had many nasty ones, but
even when a horse gives you a real bonecrusher
you'd usually still ride him again.

    It's amazing there aren't more serious falls than
there are.

Maybe – but with one in eight steeplechase rides ending in a
fall (a mere one in twenty-seven over hurdles), there are
enough to cause those of us who observe National Hunt
racing from the safer side of the running rail to marvel at the
fortitude of jump jockeys, to scratch our heads in wondrous
admiration of men and women who can find themselves
propelled into a whirl of tumbling horseflesh and flailing
hooves, then get up, swear, and start the long trek back to
base to change into the colours for their next ride.

Technically speaking, a jockey hits the deck as a result of

any one of three events. There is a 'fall' – when the horse himself hits the ground; there is 'unseated rider' – when the horse does not actually fall but negotiates the obstacle in such a way that the rider cannot maintain his seat; and there is 'brought down' – when the horse, landing over a fence, finds his path obstructed by another runner falling in front of him and cannot himself keep his feet. The distinctions are significant for the form book and your pride; but all three can hurt.

Time was when jump jockeys would merrily continue to ride despite having incurred injuries – broken bones included – which would have any normal person laid up for a month. In the modern sport that daredevil attitude is no longer deemed appropriate, and the Jockey Club provides guidelines to prevent the effect of injuries being compounded by a return to the saddle too soon after a bad fall. For example, if a jockey suffers concussion at all he must be signed off for seven days. If he is unconscious for more than three minutes, that lay-off period is extended to twenty-one days – as Tony McCoy discovered after a fall at Uttoxeter in March 1997, a spell out of action which caused him to miss the Grand National.

Tales of the jockeys of olden days riding races with broken collarbones, broken ribs, broken ankles are testimony not just to the Corinthian spirit – though there was, and is, plenty of that – but also to harsh economic necessity. Until fairly recently, no rides meant no income. Today, for protection against loss of earnings while signed off through injury, all professional jockeys have the benefit of the Professional Riders' Insurance Scheme, administered by the Jockeys' Association. Financed principally by mandatory payments from racehorse owners, who pay a percentage of every riding fee into its fund, the Scheme makes a weekly payment to every sidelined jockey, the amount based on a scale which relates to how many rides he or she had the previous season. In addition, there are capital benefits covering a range of eventualities: death, permanent total disablement and so on, down to 'extensive urinary tract damage requiring ureteric re-implantation'.

Most professional jockeys (Guy among them) supplement PRIS with a private insurance scheme while they are riding. However, insurance premiums are not cheap, and cover may have its limits. An additional safety net is provided by the Injured Jockeys' Fund, founded in 1964 in the wake of career-ending injuries suffered by two famed jump jockeys, Paddy Farrell and Tim Brookshaw (whose most memorable feat was coming a narrow second on Wyndburgh in the 1959 Grand National despite the fact that one of his stirrup leathers had broken at Becher's Brook second time round and he had had to ride the last mile and a half of the race without stirrups). Now the most popular charity in racing, the Fund provides help – financial and practical – for jockeys and their dependants whose lives have been irrevocably altered by racing injuries.

There are a good few of those. Think of Jonathan Haynes, paralysed from the waist down after being pinned under his dead horse in a Southwell seller in January 1980. Think of Sharron Murgatroyd, wheelchair-bound after breaking her neck at Bangor-on-Dee on the opening day of the 1991–2 season, whose book *Jump Jockeys Don't Cry* provided an inspirational account of the risks of her profession. Or of amateur rider Jessica Charles-Jones, also wheelchair-bound after breaking her back in a fall at Southwell.

Those are among the extreme examples of how a fall can shatter a life, but to other jockeys serious injury is almost routine. Consider the accident-prone career of Carl Llewellyn, now one of the senior riders in the weighing room:

3 September 1986: broke jaw and right cheekbone: out of action for three months;

7 November 1988: broke left forearm: out for two months;

3 March 1990: compound fracture of right ankle: out for six months;

28 August 1990: hairline fracture of left wrist, plus surgery on dislocated elbow: out for two months;

17 March 1993: broke left collarbone: out for two weeks;

30 March 1994: broke left ankle: out until August;

10 November 1994: broke right ankle and foot: out until 9 December;

9 December 1994 (yes, the very day he returned from the last one): fractured two vertebrae: out for four months.

If that catalogue of mishap is the debit side of Carl Llewellyn's career, on the credit side is a moment of riding glory which few jump jockeys ever attain, one which never came the way of such familiar names as Terry Biddlecombe or Josh Gifford or John Francome or Jonjo O'Neill or Peter Scudamore. He rode the winner of the Grand National: Party Politics in 1992.

Yet even in the moment of Party Politics' Aintree victory, the savage effect which injury can have on a jump jockey's prospects was poignantly present: the horse's regular rider was Andy Adams, who would have ridden Party Politics in the race had he not been sidelined after a fall, and whose generally low-key career would have been given a huge boost by winning the National. Fate can be particularly cruel in robbing the journeymen riders of their rare opportunities to take centre stage.

The 1996–7 jumping season furnished plenty more evidence of how Fate can deal its hand to the riding fraternity, with two of the very top riders being laid up for long periods. Mark Dwyer broke his elbow at Kelso in December and did not ride again for the whole term, and a fall at Leicester in February saw Adrian Maguire joining him on the sidelines for the rest of the season after breaking his arm. And there was no better example of the highs and lows of the sport than the experience of Tony Dobbin, who on 7 April won the Grand National and one week later had a fall at Hexham which brought his season to a premature end.

However, these misfortunes pale into insignificance behind what happened to the Irish jockey Shane Broderick (best known for his partnership with the brilliant chaser Dorans Pride), paralysed following a fall at Fairyhouse in March which resulted in a severe injury to his spinal cord. He is likely to be permanently disabled.

Monday 17 March
Still very stiff and sore, but no rides today. I've had a massage and taken some painkillers so should be OK for tomorrow: four rides at Uttoxeter, and I haven't had four rides in one day for ages. The fall apart, things are definitely looking up – just shows what riding a couple of winners can do.

Tuesday 18 March

Rode out three lots for Bill Clay this morning, then to Uttoxeter with high expectations. I was interviewed by Robert Cooper on the Racing Channel: you should ride a double today, Guy, he said. Ha bloody ha!

Riverbank Rose, one of my winners last week, was flat out from the word go and finished fourth: Bill had said not to be too hard on her if she couldn't win. She'll win again, but she needs longer than today's two miles.

Then Curragh Peter in the novice chase. What a disaster! Two of the top horses in the race were withdrawn, which seemed to give me a squeak of a chance. I intended not to make the running but to keep quite handy in the early stages, and lined up down the middle of the track. The horse nearly pulled my arms out going to the first, and jumped badly to the left, as he is prone to do, careering into another horse and knocking me sideways. My reins fell out of my hands, went around his head and got stuck up around his ears, and as he carries his head close to the ground anyway I couldn't retrieve them. The second fence was not very far after the first, and there I was charging towards it with no reins. I was lying over the horse's head and neck trying desperately to get the reins and managed to grab them just before the fence, but it was too late: he swerved and ran out. I don't think the owners and trainer were very impressed.

Beechfield Flyer, my next, was second favourite but disappointed and finished sixth, though beaten only about three lengths. Annoying, as I thought he'd win.

My last ride – picked up as a spare the day before – was Kyle David, for Frank Jordan in the novice hurdle. A great big and very green horse, he started at 100–1, but ran well for the first circuit, just behind the leaders; then he showed his greenness by failing to respond when the others quickened away from him. He got increasingly remote from the rest of the field, so I pulled him up with three hurdles to go, but the owner seemed quite pleased as that was the furthest the horse had yet managed! I suggested they turn the horse out for a year, as he's only a five-year-old and about seventeen hands tall, and needs time to develop.

Wednesday 19 March
Never mind all those fancy riding skills. What a jockey needs most is the knack of keeping in with trainers. Today I had three rides at Ludlow – Night Boat and Riverbank Red for Bill Clay, and Sandville Lad, an outsider in the bumper. I thought Night Boat might win but didn't hold out much hope for Riverbank Red, and when my father's cousin phoned and asked me to ride Mr Snaggle, in whom he owns a part, in Riverbank Red's race, I was keen to accept, as Mr Snaggle had a real chance and Riverbank Red had none. When I told Bill I didn't want to ride his, he was not amused: if you don't ride Riverbank Red, you don't ride Night Boat. Fair enough: I rode both.

Night Boat ran well. Two out I was in the lead and thought I was going to win but Chief Mouse came and caught us at the last. We finished second.

*Riverbank Red fell at the second last in her race –
won by (of course) Mr Snaggle. I'm a bit pissed off at
having to turn down the ride on a winner, but that's the
way it goes. Sandville Lad in the bumper ran a blinder:
50–1, we led most of the way until headed in the last
quarter mile. Finished second. The owners were thrilled.*

Saturday 22 March
*Just as well I didn't get on the wrong side of Bill Clay
over Night Boat the other day, as he brought the horse
out again today in the conditional jockeys' hurdle at
Bangor. I kept the ride – and won. Night Boat started
favourite and we took the lead coming to the last: I just
had to ride him out to win by three lengths from an
outsider named Nord Lys.*

*My fourth winner of the season, and my third in the
last twelve days. I wonder how far behind Tony
McCoy I am now . . .*

*Prussia, first time out since the Cheltenham Festival,
ran in a handicap hurdle – much more his level – and
put in a terrific performance. He led after the last and I
thought he was going to hold on, then along comes
Richard Dunwoody on a David Gandolfo horse called
Selatan, pips us on the line and wins a neck. It was a
typical Dunwoody performance, and as I hammered
for the line I knew it was him coming up behind from
the growling! Everybody says what a gentle, quietly
spoken, articulate guy Richard is, but hear him growl
at his horse in a close finish and you'll get another
side to him. It works, though.*

Bill Clay was chuffed to bits by Prussia's run: his horses seem to be coming into form, and I've every chance of a few more winners from the yard.

Two more rides at Bangor for Pam Whittle, for whom I've been riding out recently: she has around twenty-five horses in her yard and seems like an up-and-coming trainer. Ledburian, a great big long boat of a horse, started at 100–1 in the maiden chase and pulled up. Her other runner was Rocky Balboa, 50–1 in the bumper. There was chaos at the start as the starter let us go while half the field were still trying to get into position, but I wasn't affected, and got away OK: to no avail though, as we were tailed off.

Having to ride all these bad horses, horses with no apparent chance whatsoever, annoys me sometimes, as I know I'm perfectly capable of doing much better if I had a superior sort of animal to ride. The saying that good horses make good jockeys may be pretty trite, but it's completely true. A ride on a bad horse is not going to make the jockey look any good, but you have to keep riding them to make a living, and it's only by keeping in the thick of things that you'll be around when the chance to ride a good horse does come up.

Bad horses are my bread and butter, and though even I would turn down a ride if I knew it to be terminally bonkers, I can't afford to do that too often. Once Graham Thorner phoned me to ride one of his, but he warned me that it would belt a few fences and was 'not a lad's ride', and he wouldn't be put out if I declined. As it would have been my only ride that *day and I knew this horse to be extremely dodgy, I declined. Graham was as nice as pie about it, and said he quite understood. Robbie Supple took the ride: the horse fell at the first fence, breaking Robbie's wrist. It's your own choice whether to ride the dodgy ones or not, but it helps to be aware that there are two different kinds of bad horse: bad useless and bad horrible. The bad useless ones will just be slow. The bad horrible will put you in hospital.*

Pam Whittle has asked me to ride for her at Ludlow on Monday, but Sunday evening I'm going to London for the annual jockeys' awards dinner, the Lesters. Normally most of us stay up all night and don't move – never mind getting up – on Monday morning, so the idea of having to make my way up to Ludlow to ride in the novice chase is very unappealing. I told Pam that I wouldn't be in any fit state to ride and she's been very understanding.

Monday 24 March
Lucky I'd got out of riding at Ludlow today. I'd never have made it up there after last night's revels in London – and the horse I was supposed to ride in the novice chase pulled up.

Had a wonderful time at the Lesters – practically the only social occasion of the year when the jump jockeys and Flat jockeys get together. I used to be great mates with Jason Weaver, who lived near me in South Wales, then when he went off to join Luca Cumani in Newmarket we mostly lost touch, so it's good to see him once a year at the Lesters. In the early hours of the morning, after the dinner and presentation of awards at the Hilton, a group of us left to make our way back to the Kensington Close Hotel to round things off, as usual, with a few games of pool and a raucous sing-song. On our way there we bought some celebrity masks from a souvenir shop which for some reason was open at four-thirty in the morning. We put these on (I was the Queen) and marched into what we thought was the Kensington Close Hotel – only it wasn't, and the management of wherever we had ended up discreetly asked us to leave. Out on the street again we spent half an hour looking for the right hotel, then had to resort to a passing taxi – only to find that our destination was just round the corner. By the time we got there we'd sobered up and the joke with the masks had worn off. Got to bed some time between six and seven, though many of the lads didn't bother with bed at all. Trainers are very understanding about jockeys' difficulty getting up this one morning of the year, and tend to let them off early-morning duties today – though David Nicholson had insisted that John Kavanagh be at the yard at crack of dawn this morning to school his Grand National mount Turning Trix, before coming clean at the last minute just before John set off for the Lesters and reassuring him that it was all a wind-up!

Plenty of sore heads around the racecourses today, and a good few horses running away with their jockeys on the way down to the start, their riders in no fit state to take full control.

Tuesday 25 March
*Curragh Peter in a handicap chase at Southwell. He
had ten stone – nine eleven with my allowance – and
after the excesses of the weekend I had to sit in the
sauna for ages last night. The Clerk of the Scales let me
through at nine twelve, one pound overweight. That
pound didn't make much difference to Curragh Peter,
but he ran a good race to finish second, though way
behind the winner, at 25–1.*

*Most of the horses I'm riding at the moment are
running as well as they can. Things aren't going too
bad.*

Saturday 29 March
*I'd been offered a ride at Newton Abbot on Jay Jay's
Voyage, and then lost it. The horse's trainer John
Scrivens had asked me to go down and ride him out,
but I couldn't as I was committed too heavily to other
people, so Tom Dascombe went and rode him out, and
got the ride. I wasn't too bothered: Jay Jay's Voyage is
fourteen – very long in the tooth for a racehorse –
hadn't run for ages and seemed to have little chance at
Newton Abbot; and in any case I was supposed to be
going to Plumpton to ride a horse who appeared to
have much better prospects.*

*This was Against The Clock in the conditional
jockeys' handicap hurdle, for Peter Bowen. I'd never
ridden for him before but he's an up-and-coming
trainer, and it's always good to make a new connection.
Went to Plumpton via Heathrow, where I was*

dropping off a Czech friend; then two hours' sleep in the car at a hotel near at the course and a spell in the hotel's sauna. Against The Clock finished fifth.

Jay Jay's Voyage won his race.

That Mr Snaggle – whom I could have ridden last week – has just won again at Towcester. I wasn't asked to ride him this time, but had I ridden him last time I probably would have been. You win some, you lose some.

It's the Grand National a week today and I haven't got a ride, which is a bit of a drag. I loved riding in it last year and would ride anything. I've been hoping to get on an outsider, just to have a run round, but at the moment it doesn't look as if there'll be many runners, as there's no rain and the ground is coming up firm everywhere.

In fact, with the going the way it is, a lot of the trainers I ride for aren't running their horses anywhere. Still, as long as Bill Clay keeps putting me up I should be all right for rides for the next few weeks.

Monday 31 March
Bank Holiday Monday. Five rides at Uttoxeter, my busiest day of the season so far. Felt that all of them had a squeak, but drew a blank.

The first two were for Bill Clay. Saymore finished fourth, then in a novices' handicap hurdle Beechfield Flyer made a terrific race of it with the favourite El Freddie, trained by Jim Old. We chased him all the way home, and were beaten a neck.

*Next up, in a novices' chase, was Fox Chapel, who
in his time had been a very good horse: now a ten-
year-old in Rod Juckes' yard, he'd been trained on the
Flat by Richard Hannon and later by Jimmy
FitzGerald. As a three-year-old he'd even won the
Britannia Handicap at Royal Ascot at 100–1, but by
now he was a real character. I'd ridden him before in a
hurdle, but not in a chase. He's never normally on the
bridle, but today he travelled really well in the early
part of the race, and put in a great round of jumping.
Coming past the stands with one circuit to go he
dropped the bit for a stride or two – horses often do
that when they reckon they've done enough, or are
passing the stable area and think they can go back for
a rest – and I picked my stick up and gave him a
couple of quick backhanders. He was not impressed
by this treatment and started dogging it, but as soon as
I put my stick down it fell out of my hand – the first
time in my life I've ever dropped my stick in a race.
There I was, sitting on the biggest rogue around, with
a circuit to go and nothing to wake him up with.
In the event it didn't matter: within seconds, going
past the bottom bend by the stands, Fox Chapel
broke down badly on both front legs and I pulled
him up.*

The Thoroughbred horse may appear to be an animal of
huge strength, but centuries of selective breeding, instilling
into it speed and the frame of mind to deploy that speed,
have also made it a delicate creature, subject to all sorts of

stresses and strains. Galloping places the horse's legs under considerable pressure, and the tendons in the foreleg – which attach the muscles above the knee to the pastern and pedal bones in the foot – are put under extra strain when jumping. Uneven going, tired muscles and severe impact on the legs (as when landing over a jump at thirty miles an hour) all increase the likelihood of tendon strain, and in extreme cases the tendons elongate or give way completely: this is what is commonly known as 'breaking down'.

To the spectator the first sign that a horse has broken down is that he will falter in his gallop and his stride will shorten. If this happens towards the climax of the race, his spirit may enable him to keep going despite the pain. (Indeed, distressing as the sight of a hobbling horse may be to spectators, there is plenty of veterinary evidence that the horse does not feel the worst of the pain at the time injury strikes. As a beast of flight, the instinct to escape his pursuer temporarily overrides sensation in the injured limb.) There are plenty of instances of horses who have valiantly raced on after those tendons have given way under the strain: perhaps the most famous example in modern steeplechasing history is when the great chaser Mandarin won the Grand Steeplechase de Paris under Fred Winter in 1962 despite the fact that (a) his bit had broken early on in the race so that his jockey had no steering, and (b) the horse had broken down three fences from home.

To the jockey that unmistakable feeling that your horse has 'gone' is one of the more upsetting occupational hazards.

Often the first sign that a horse is about to break down is that he will change his legs – alter the pattern of his stride – in reaction to the discomfort. Within a few seconds Fox Chapel went from galloping normally to hobbling and then virtually falling over. Horses can recover from severe tendon injuries, but Fox Chapel was so badly damaged that later he had to be put down.

My next at Uttoxeter was a spare ride – Dark Oak in the three-mile handicap chase. He'd been a good horse on his day but was now eleven and on the downward slope. Derek Byrne had been booked to ride him, but had got dehydrated by wasting and had to cry off. In the race, the horse just didn't want to know: he never went a yard, though even so he finished third because two of the other four runners unseated their riders three out.

Tuesday 1 April
A trainer (who had better remain nameless) has blown me out this morning. I used to ride all his horses and now, though he only has four or five, he still expects me to go and ride them out. I couldn't do it. He had two runners at Newton Abbot on Saturday and wouldn't let me ride them as I hadn't been able to go down and school them. I was busy elsewhere, but probably he wasn't worth riding for anyway. I don't want to fall out with him, but I have my doubts as to whether he'll be putting me up on his horses again, at least for the immediate future.

Trainers can be like that. They expect too much from you, and sometimes you're better off keeping

*your distance. Ride out for them a few times – unpaid,
remember – and they expect you down there all the
time.*

*Uttoxeter again today. Night Boat was disap-
pointing, finishing fourth. Bill Clay had told me to
drop right out, then come with a late run. The leaders
went very quick and just didn't stop, so that when I
made my move two out I was never going to catch
them. Had I laid up handier I possibly would have
been second, but I'd never have beaten the winner.*

*Most jockeys can make up their own minds about
how to ride a race if they know enough about the
horse, and they have to be able to adapt to how the
race is run. When they're told to ride the race in such
and such a way by the trainer they normally do it, but
on this occasion I rather wish I hadn't listened, as I
might have finished closer if I had ridden my own
race.*

*Rode Test Match in the handicap hurdle. When we
got down to the start I thought he was lame, but
having decided to let him take his chance, I had to
pull him up after a mile as he was hating the firmish
ground: his action went, and had we gone any further
I think he would have broken down.*

*Jasons Farm – the bugger who trod on my eye at
Hereford – is a complete yak. He started at 100–1 in
the maiden hurdle (a pretty skinny price in my opinion)
and was back-pedalling after a mile. He was tailed off
but I got him round: he's got so many Ps (for Pulled
Up) and Fs (for Fell) in his form line, I thought it*

*would be nice for him to have a number by his name
for a change, even if it's just 0 (for unplaced).*

Wednesday 2 April
*Three days before the National and I'm still trying to
find a ride, but at this stage there's not much prospect.
Most of the runners are jocked up already, and
although I've spent some time phoning round on the
chance of getting on one of the lower-weighted horses,
it looks like Hereford, not Aintree, for me on Saturday.*

*Another ride for Pam Whittle: Ledburian again, this
time in the novice chase at Worcester. Starting a 66–1
outsider, he picked up right out of my hands at the
open ditch, took off from outside the wings, landed
halfway across the fence and gave me no chance.
Buried me. I wasn't concussed but my head was sore
for a while afterwards. Pam Whittle, far from being
annoyed, just kept laughing at me when I got back
to the weighing room.*

Saturday 5 April
*Grand National day. Last year I was in the thick of the
action with my ride on Brackenfield, one of the great
experiences of my riding life – not just the race itself,
but all the build-up as well. I was billed as the youngest
jockey in the race (and would have been had Rodney
Farrant not had a fall at Ludlow the day before the
National and been replaced on Riverside Boy by David
Walsh, who's a few weeks younger than me). I
attracted lots of publicity: articles about me in the*

*press, pieces on the radio and (though I suppose I
should blush to admit it) a feature in the* Daily Sport.

This was the idea of my sister Zoë, who phoned the
Sport *and told them that my ambition was to meet a
Page Three girl. Before I knew it I was in a park near
the course, wearing colours (actually the colours I wore
on Channel Pastime in the John Hughes two days
before the National), and smiling for a photographer
with – yes! – a blonde lady wearing very little in the
way of clothing. Her name was Rachel, and she sat
astride me (squeamish readers skip a few paragraphs)
as I knelt on all fours and she posed as if giving me a
couple with the whip. This scene must have offended
some of the locals, as after a few minutes our photo
session was abruptly brought to a halt when a police
helicopter flew over and Rachel was told to get
her clothes on.*

*But the photographer had got enough, and Rachel
and I duly appeared in glorious colour on the front
page of the* Daily Sport *and again – with her wearing
even less – inside the paper.*

If Guy's fifteen minutes of fame came at a price, this was it.

The panel on the front page of the *Daily Sport* announced
that on page two readers would find a 'Grand National
Exclusive' about Guy, Rachel and the police helicopter – or,
to put it in *Sport*-speak, 'Big chopper shocker for Page 3 girl
havin' jump with jockey – by Rachel Travers riding Guy
Lewis riding Brackenfield at 66–1 in National!' Turn to page
two for the full story:

Page Three stunna Rachel Travis was rudely interrupted by a chopper yesterday when she hitched a lift with Grand National jockey and avid *Daily Sport* fan Guy Lewis.

As the frisky 36–24–36 filly straddled the rider of 66–1 shot Brackenfield, a police helicopter hovered overhead. And a voice boomed through a loudspeaker: 'Stop riding that jockey and put your clothes back on.'

Guy, 21, the youngest jockey in the big race, is set to achieve his life's ambition when he steers his mount over Aintree's awesome fences.

And he revealed his second major goal: 'I'd love to take a naked Page Three girl round the course on my back.' . . .

In an attempt to introduce a measure of gravitas into the proceedings, the *Daily Sport* squeezed a quote out of – who else? – 'Channel Four's wacky pundit John McCririck', who pronounced:

'What a great idea it would be to have a Page Three National.

'Just think, we could have Page Three girls jumping over fences TOPLESS.

'And I could be one of the fences!'

After all that sort of larking about, the Grand National itself was pretty straightforward. I wasn't nervous as I'd already got round the course two days earlier on

Channel Pastime, so I knew what the fences held in store, and riding a 100–1 shot to whom nobody gave an earthly chance meant that there was no pressure at all. Some of the papers had said ominous things about Brackenfield, about how it would take a brave man to ride him in the National as he was renowned for belting his fences, but often Aintree brings about a transformation in a dodgy jumper, and I wasn't that worried.

The atmosphere in the weighing room before the race was tremendous – everybody very keyed up, lots of good luck cards, a great sense of occasion and excitement. All the family came up to support me: even on a 100–1 outsider, a ride in the National is something very special.

It wasn't only the press who were aware of Brackenfield's problem with his jumping. The other jockeys asked me whether I'd go down the inner or the outer, as none of them wanted to get in behind me and risk interference. Even Brackenfield's trainer Paul Nicholls didn't have much faith. He had another runner in the race, the strongly fancied Deep Bramble, and his main instructions to me were to keep out of Deep Bramble's way! Beyond that, he said not to ask him any serious questions at the fences, and just go out and enjoy yourself, and that's what I did.

We were bumped and bored a bit over the first two fences, then settled down into the rhythm of the race and took up a nice position in mid-division. Coming towards the end of the first circuit we'd moved up to

track the leaders, and at the Chair – the huge open
ditch in front of the stands – I gave Brackenfield a kick
and asked him to attack it: one!, two!, three!, and he
picked up and jumped it brilliantly. At this point I
started to think that if I could keep up with the leaders,
then put him in front around second Becher's, he might
lead them to the second last and stay on to finish
fourth or fifth. He wouldn't have the speed to cope
with a horse like Rough Quest, who'd finished a good
second in the Cheltenham Gold Cup. Still, nothing
ventured, nothing gained, and going out into the
country for the second circuit I started to pick up a few
places. We jumped the seventeenth fine, then the
eighteenth, and the next was the great big open ditch,
which catches out so many horses when it's jumped as
the third fence on the first circuit. Having successfully
one! two! three!-ed Brackenfield into the Chair, I
repeated the formula. One! Two! Three! . . . But this
time he said Four!, put his hind legs in the ditch and hit
the fence as if it were a brick wall. There was no way I
could stay on after that and off I pitched. Unseated
rider.

Brackenfield had a few scratches but was otherwise
none the worse for wear. I was a bit annoyed with
myself, as I felt that if I hadn't asked him the question
at that nineteenth fence he would probably have found
his own way to the other side. Maybe I should have sat
back on him and taken a pull, but the pace was quickening and I didn't want to go into the fence in fourth
place and come out of it in seventh or eighth. These are

the sort of calculations you have to make in an instant in any race, be it the Grand National or a conditional riders' novice hurdle at Hereford – which is the very race in which, after all the excitement of Grand National day 1996, I was destined to ride on Grand National day 1997.

Nuns Lucy had ten stone and I knew I'd need a good bout in the sauna as soon as I got to the races. The horse is trained by Frank Jordan, for whom I'd ridden out not long ago. I wanted to make sure I could do the weight on the horse, so I was horrified when I weighed myself on arrival at the course: ten stone three! If I was going to do ten stone for my ride – in the last race of the day – that meant I had to lose six pounds in about three hours. Some of the other jockeys said I couldn't possibly do it, but I had to have a go.

The race was due off at five twenty-five. I went into the sauna around two o'clock, and sat and suffered. The weight just poured off me, and by the time the Grand National was due to start I was down to nine stone eleven stripped – the right weight for riding at ten stone.

I got out of the sauna to watch the National on the weighing room television, and discovered what had been happening at Aintree. Oh shit!, I thought, and went back into the sauna again until it was time to get dressed and weigh out – which I duly did at ten stone.

Nuns Lucy pulled up. Six pounds sweated off in three hours: was it worth it?

What had caused the Lewis exclamation of 'Oh shit!' was one of the most extraordinary episodes in the long, distinguished and occasionally tortured history of the Grand National, in the public perception the biggest event of the entire racing year, Flat or National Hunt.

In prospect it had looked a good renewal of the big race. The 1996 winner Rough Quest was sidelined through injury, but the 38-runner field contained enough of the top staying chasers to ensure a race in the best traditions of the National. And tradition was a key theme at Aintree on 5 April. This was to be the 150th running of the big race, and Peter O'Sullevan, veteran BBC commentator and racing legend, was to call for the last time the event of which his voice had become an integral part. After the first three races the course was abuzz.

Thirty-five minutes before the scheduled start of the big race at 3.45, the festival atmosphere of National Day was shattered. Some of the runners were being led round the parade ring, others were still in the saddling boxes, when over the public address system came the instruction that the crowd were to evacuate the stands area and make their way over to the inside of the track. Security alert. The spectators' compliance with this request was initially casual, accompanied by a communal shrug of the shoulders: oh well, better do what they say, but the National will be late off. It was only when a subsequent public address exhortation to keep evacuating all areas was accompanied by the insistence that 'this is very serious' that the mood changed. A degree of urgency was instilled, and within half an hour the entire population of the racecourse – spectators, owners, trainers, jockeys, catering staff clutching their till drawers, bookmakers, the Tote's ladies in red, gatemen, the lot – had decamped, as far away as possible from the stands. The horses about to run in the Grand National had been hastily taken back to their stables, and all course buildings and all car parks were sealed off as police started their search for the devices which, according to coded telephoned warnings, had been hidden on the course.

Any lingering hope that the 70,000 spectators would get to see the Grand National soon evaporated, and by five o'clock the bemused thousands were milling around outside the racecourse, hoping to get their cars out.

Then from a police helicopter – the same one that had disturbed the frolics of Page Three stunna Rachel? – came the bellowed announcement that the car parks would not be opened that night:

'Make your own way home!'

'We can't!' shouted the crowd back in a futile gesture of frustration: 'Our cars are in there!'

The horses were allowed to be moved out (some took refuge at Haydock Park racecourse), and as the crowds eventually accepted the situation and dispersed to try to find lodgings for the night, traditional Liverpool hospitality came into its own, with local residents opening their doors – and the doors of their spare bedrooms – to stranded racegoers. Student halls of residence were commandeered; sports and leisure centres became emergency dormitories.

A group of weary journalists made their way to the Moat House Hotel in the centre of Liverpool, to discover – not to their great surprise – that all rooms had been taken for the night. But reception staff at the Moat House were phoning round other hotels in the area in an attempt to get refugees billeted where they could.

'A hotel in Chester has three rooms, £39.50 each,' reported a receptionist after making another mercy phone call.

'We'll take them!' sang out the battle-scarred hacks, and the receptionist returned to the phone to confirm the booking – only to return to the scribes with the news that the rooms had suddenly gone up to £100 each.

Clearly the milk of human kindness, dispensed by the tanker-load in Liverpool itself, was in short supply over the county border.

The car parks were not reopened until late on the Sunday afternoon, by which time Grand National day 1997 had already entered the history books as one of the most bizarre sporting occasions of all – its oddity no better summed up than by what happened to the jockeys.

The weighing room before the Grand National has an atmosphere all its own, an air of expectancy and excitement unlike that at any other time. In 1997 that atmosphere was cruelly punctured. All keyed up and ready to go out to the parade ring before the National – Richard Dunwoody, rider of Smith's Band, was having his cap tied by valet John Buckingham when the alarm sounded – the jockeys were hastily ordered out with no opportunity to change out of their riding silks (or their wafer-soled riding boots), and had to join the milling throngs in the mass evacuation. When the police declined to allow anyone at all access to the course buildings, the jockeys – told, like everyone else, to come back tomorrow – were forced to fend for themselves. A group of them made their way across to the nearby house where John Buckingham was staying for the meeting, to be plied with sandwiches, tea and stronger drink. Another batch found haven in a Runcorn hotel, transported there by trainer (and former jockey) Simon Earle in the horsebox carrying his Grand National hope Dextra Dove. Some made for the Moat House, by early evening awash with Aintree strays, and improvised: one room there was reputed to have slept seventeen. (Jamie Osborne, due to ride one of the hottest fancies for the race in Suny Bay, later related how at a central Liverpool train station a local wag, seeing the jockey in his riding colours, shouted across: 'Oi, mate – you come here straight from work?')

Many of the jockeys who had found shelter in one of the city centre hotels settled in for an impromptu night on the booze – or some other activity, if the boasts of a blonde lady on a public telephone in the Adelphi the following morning are to be taken at face value – and throughout that Sunday morning the sight of jump jockeys still clad in their colours congregating on street corners or wandering in and out of the Adelphi lobby provided a bizarre emblem of Grand National day 1997.

The race was eventually run on the Monday, and won in brilliant style by Lord Gyllene, ridden by Tony Dobbin.

Monday 7 April
The Grand National was being run this afternoon, but most of the riding arrangements were as they were on Saturday, and still there was nothing for me in the race.

Saturday 12 April

To Newton Abbot to ride the fourteen-year-old Jay Jay's Voyage – a bit of a granddad, but then, he won last time. It wasn't a very good race today and I thought I had a squeak, though the horse was coming back from a long layoff – two years – when he won at Newton Abbot, and sometimes after that sort of time off they don't reproduce their form second time out. Today's trip of two miles was probably too sharp, as the leaders were always that bit quick for him. But he stayed on to finish fourth.

There weren't many runners at Newton Abbot today, as the ground is so hard at the moment that many trainers aren't willing to risk their horses. Bill Clay seems to be giving his a couple of easy weeks, and it's going to be a struggle getting rides over the next few weeks. It's the same for every jockey, but it's particularly aggravating for me at the moment as over the last couple of months things have started looking up: lots of rides, three winners. I really need to keep up that momentum.

Tuesday 15 April

Exeter. Rode Station Express in the conditional jockeys' handicap hurdle. He was a 50–1 chance and Tom Dascombe was on a 33–1 shot, and we had a little bet between ourselves to see who would beat whom. Mine was tailed off four from home, but then his started to come back to me. All the horses around us had pulled up or were just cantering gently back, but I got my horse going again and came charging up behind Tom at the last, screaming at him that I was going to beat him. We watched the replay later, and sure enough could see these two idiots pushing the heads off their horses in sixth and seventh place. I actually gave my fellow a couple of backhanders – which was stupid, considering the stewards watch every move you make, and you don't normally give your horse a smack when you're beaten. Tom ended up winning our private race by about a length, so I had to stand him a couple of pints later.

Saturday 19 April
Today held the prospect of a few rides as the top jockeys are at Ayr for the Scottish National, but in the event I had just the two at Bangor. Prussia started second favourite but ran an absolute stinker. He pulled hard for the first mile, then three out, when they quick-ened up in front of me, he dogged it – just dropped out like he'd been shot. I think he's turning into a bit of an old rogue. Curragh Peter ran all right to finish fourth in his race, not beaten too far. There's probably a bad race for him somewhere.

No rain for ages, and things are getting more and more desperate: the ground is so hard, it even looks as if Friday evening's meeting at Taunton might be called off. I'm struggling to make a living at the moment, and all I can do is ride out for some of these trainers with top-of-the-ground horses and hope for the best.

Friday 25 April
A bit of rain at last, and Taunton went ahead. One ride
there – Miss Griffin for Nick Ayliffe. Ran all right up to
the home turn, then faded.

    Watched the next race, a novices' chase, from the
stand, near the water jump. The second favourite Duke
Of Dreams, ridden by Vince Slattery, misjudged the
fence and dragged his hind legs through the water.
Vince pulled him up immediately but the horse was
clearly very badly hurt: probably broke his back.
He was quickly put down. Horrible.

The death of horses in action is an unavoidable aspect of
jump racing. About 0.5 per cent of horses competing in
National Hunt races – 1 in 200 – are either killed outright or
put down on the course, through a variety of causes: a heart
attack suffered during a race; a broken back, neck or leg,
after blundering at a jump; a leg snapping while racing on the
flat. For a jockey the act of pulling the saddle off a dead or
irreparably injured horse and trudging back to the weighing
room as the distraught connections rush to give the animal
comfort is one of the most distressing experiences of a riding
life.

In all my races under Rules I've only ever once had
a horse die. I was still an amateur, and was riding
Up-A-Point at Newton Abbot for Philip Hobbs. He
was in about fifth place, travelling well just off the
pace, and needed one nice jump to bring him up to the
leaders' heels. He met the fence spot-on but never took

off and crashed through, breaking his neck on landing. The vets thought he'd probably had a heart attack just before he took off. I half blamed myself for asking him to go long, but if he had indeed had a heart attack I suppose it wouldn't have made any difference what I was asking him.

To have a horse die under you is a pretty unpleasant experience, but you don't get that attached to most horses you ride, and you just have to accept it and get on with thinking about the next race.

Friday 2 May
Bangor, after a few days out of action with tonsillitis. Rode Riverbank Rose in the three-mile hurdle: finished fifth. Bangor is a tight track, and three miles round there involves enough circuits of the course to make you dizzy at the best of times. After a spell sick in bed I was finding it difficult to concentrate on how many times round we had to go, but I managed not to disgrace myself.

Saturday 3 May
Kadari's first race over fences, at Uttoxeter: she finished fourth. Then Night Boat in the novice chase. He made a mess of the third, then at the seventh took off a mile too soon and never had any chance of clearing the fence properly. He left his back legs on the wrong side and drilled me into the ground. He then stood on my wrist as he got up, and it looks as if he might have ended my season. The wrist came up like a balloon; the

course doctor said it looked broken and suggested I go
to the hospital in Stafford, so I drove myself over there.
It was a quiet afternoon in casualty and I was able to
get looked at fairly quickly: they X-rayed the wrist and
said it was badly bruised, but not broken. I drove
home with one hand and in extreme discomfort.

Wednesday 7 May
I didn't ride Monday (Bank Holiday) or yesterday, but
rather than take the whole week off dosed myself up
with painkillers and went and rode Strike-A-Pose for
Bernard Llewellyn at Chepstow. The horse seemed to
have quite a good chance, but ran disappointingly.
After the race I saw the course doctor and he stood me
down for a few days, so I should be able to claim a
bit off the jockeys' insurance.

Saturday 10 May
The end of an eventful week.
    Bill Clay has told me that he'll probably only have
eight or ten horses next season, which isn't enough to
keep me very busy: I really need a regular supply from
a trainer with thirty or forty in the yard. Frank Jordan
was a possibility a few weeks ago: perhaps I should go
and have a round of golf with him to talk about the
chances, though at the moment my wrist isn't really up
to golf.
    Rides this season have really dried up, and lots of us
are struggling to get by. Every jockey tries to stay free
of injury, but at this time of year a little injury is not

*entirely unwelcome, and I've found myself wishing that
I had indeed broken my wrist. A few weeks off, paid
for by the Professional Riders' Insurance Scheme,
would have been just the job!*

Sunday 11 May
*At times like this I wonder what's going to happen. I'm
riding horses which I might manage to avoid if I had a
greater choice. Many of the horses that run during the
summer months aren't much good, but a bad horse can
win a bad race, as long as it can go on top of the
ground.*

*Perhaps I should find a part-time job that I could
do when not riding – something that would keep me
occupied, bring in a few quid, stop me sitting around
getting bored and eating. So long as I can get a few
rides a week I have the motivation to keep my
weight down.*

*There are bills to be paid for the car, plus MOT,
then there's road tax: at least £500 in all. And I need to
change my car. The mileage on it is astronomical, and
if I don't get rid of it now it won't be worth threepence
in six months' time.*

*It always seem that when things slacken on the rides
front, that's when the bills start to come flooding in.*

Sod's law.

Tuesday 13 May
*Rode a horse called Prerogative for Gary Moore at
Chepstow: 20–1, tailed off. (Was that worth coming*

back from injury for?) But he's the sort of horse who should be running a few times through the summer.

Wednesday 14 May
Two at Hereford. Both ran badly.

But Peter Scudamore phoned today and asked if I could go over to ride in Norway or Sweden during the summer – probably once a week. The money's good and it will be a useful experience. I'm going to the Czech Republic again in June, so after all there'll be enough riding to prevent me sitting round on my arse all summer.

Thursday 15 May
After racing at Hereford yesterday I stayed with Dai Tegg at the pub he manages between Ledbury and Hereford. Dai has been a good friend of mine since the time I was first riding, and I learned a great deal from him. He had a couple of bad falls and kept on riding, and then had a brain haemorrhage and had to give up. It's taken him a very long time to recover, and I suppose he's lucky to be alive. But to be honest he's not the same Dai I used to know: he gets tired very quickly – especially in the evenings – and in some ways is a shadow of his former self.

Just goes to show how dangerous this job is. Makes you wonder whether it's worth it.

7

Running on Empty

*'You waste your pants off and the horse
pulls up anyway'*

DOROTHY PARKER'S FAMOUS REACTION TO reports that US President Calvin Coolidge had died, 'How do they know?', might equally apply to the end of the jumping season.

After the Grand National the season starts to dwindle towards its dotage, and following the last big chase, the Whitbread Gold Cup at Sandown Park at the end of April, it sinks deeper and deeper into its final sleep. The best horses are put away for the summer, turned out into paddocks at their trainers' yards or sent home to their owners' farms to spend the summer months quietly cropping grass and swatting flies off each others' faces with their tails. Equine athletes, no less than human, need to rest, to recharge their batteries before returning to the fray, and as the late spring and summer months wear on, the living is easy. Long days on rich pasture eradicate the memory of flogging up the Sandown Park hill in the freezing rain or sloshing through the Cheltenham mud.

The daylight hours will be shortening rapidly by the time they're brought back into serious training.

But while the equine elite take their leisure in the long days and warm nights, there is still sport for lesser animals – and the jockeys who ride them. For whereas the National Hunt season used to run from August to June, with an official two-month gap between terms, it now runs from June to June (or, as in 1997, the very end of May), with certain courses (specifically, those that can keep the ground raceable even in dry weather) staging jump meetings throughout high summer.

As the days lengthen the quality of the racing may diminish, but there are still great National Hunt occasions to be tasted, most of all on Spring Bank Holiday at the end of May, when six tracks around the country – Cartmel, Fontwell, Hereford, Huntingdon, Uttoxeter and Wetherby – stage a sort of final fling of jumping jollity. Of these, none is more jolly, nor more emblematic of the informal appeal of jump racing, than the Bank Holiday Monday meeting at Cartmel, where twenty thousand people crowd into the gloriously scenic Lakeland track, with the ancient priory standing sentinel nearby and the cosy gardens of village cottages rolling down to the running rail. You can attempt some home cooking alongside hundreds of like-minded chefs in the barbecue area, have a kickabout on the course before the equestrian action commences, enjoy the rides and games in the huge funfair in the middle of the track, or simply settle down to a picnic. What you cannot do, however carefully you pick your vantage point, is see more than a tiny portion of the racing itself; but this does not seem to matter a jot. Cartmel, like so much jump racing around the minor tracks (and they don't come much more minor than Cartmel, with only six days' racing in 1997), is less about the form book than about communal enjoyment of a day out. The racing is a major part of that fun, but not the be-all and end-all of the afternoon's revelry.

For Guy Lewis, an outing to Cartmel, one of the few British tracks where he had never ridden, would have to remain an unfulfilled ambition in 1997. His commitments kept him closer to home.

Two rides at Hereford seemed a pretty measly programme for a Bank Holiday Monday, when all those meetings should have provided lots of opportunities. But the ground had been firm and there weren't too many runners.

My first at Hereford was in the novice chase on Chan The Man, owned like Channel Pastime by Mel and Sandra Worthington. To be honest, I wasn't much looking forward to riding him as he could be very unpredictable: not a nice ride. My other was Sober Island, a horse who is no good at all. I'd had to waste really hard to do the weight on that one. I wasn't feeling too bright anyway and the wasting made me feel much worse.

It just goes to show that you shouldn't get too pessimistic. Chan The Man had got his act together and he jumped really well, went clear approaching the straight and absolutely pissed up. My fifth winner of the season. Not enough – not nearly enough – but good to have another one in the bag.

After the race I felt awful. I'd been wasting hard for Sober Island in the last, and it looked as though I'd overdone it. I felt sick and weak – so wretched, in fact, that I thought I might have to give up the ride. After about an hour lying on the bench in the weighing room I began to feel better, but was so dehydrated that I had to drink ten cups of orange squash to get some fluid back into me. This made me feel a little more human but was bound to show on the scales, and I weighed out two pounds overweight.

Sober Island started at 40–1, lost touch with the others early in the race and pulled up. You waste your pants off and the horse pulls up anyway.

Guy was not to know it that day, but Sober Island was his final ride of the 1996–7 season. Horses he had been expecting to ride at the final meetings, at Stratford on the Friday evening and Saturday afternoon and at Market Rasen on the Saturday evening – the fixture after which the season is finally pronounced dead – went to other jockeys. Horses he had won on previously were no longer offered to him.

There's no point sitting round feeling sorry for yourself. You've got to be getting up off your arse and doing something. But then you might put people off by appearing too keen. Often you're sitting at home doing nothing when the phone rings and something that you'd never expected falls into your lap – that ride which raises your hopes just when you're feeling at your lowest. You do nothing right and the opportunity comes along; you do nothing wrong, and end up being treated like shit.

The inauguration of the summer jumping programme has made the line between one season and the next a somewhat artificial division, as one term follows hard on the heels of the previous one, and for most of the professionals it's business as usual straight away. The option for a jockey to take a few weeks in the sun is still there, of course – for those who can afford it – but by the time you're unpacking your factor 10 on your return, McCoy is already twenty winners clear in the table . . .

On the Monday following the Saturday evening meeting at Market Rasen which brought down the curtain on the 1996–7 season, that same Tony McCoy dominated the page of jockeys' statistics in the *Sporting Life*. There he was winning the Gold Cup on Mr Mulligan. There he was landing the Champion Hurdle on Make A Stand. There he was posing beside the gleaming Saab convertible he had received at Stratford on the Saturday afternoon, his prize for heading the jockeys' table with 190 winners from 665 rides.

The statistics for Guy Lewis read:

141 rides
5 winners
strike rate of winners to rides: 3.5 per cent
12 seconds
12 thirds
4 falls
win prize money (for the owners): £14,517
(Guy's official cut of the prize money from the five winners came to £1,324.15)
win and place prize money (for the owners): £33,942

Even for a jockey resigned – for the moment – to his fate of riding poor horses, five winners in a season is a pretty poor haul. Tony McCoy, for heaven's sake, rode five winners on one day at Uttoxeter on Spring Bank Holiday Monday.

Nor was a total of five remotely high enough to revive concerns about what would happen to his career when he lost his three-pound claim. Any such thoughts had long since evaporated, and in any case the Jockey Club had recently announced a change whereby that three-pound allowance would remain until the rider had partnered sixty-five winners – an increase of ten over the previous threshold. Additionally, a jockey could ride as a conditional until he or she reached the age of twenty-six (up from twenty-five). At twenty-two, Guy had plenty of time, and for the moment the ability to claim the allowance longer than had been the case should, when it came to trainers dispensing rides, give him an edge over jockeys of similar standing but without the allowance.

Another telling statistic, not included in any published list, is that no fewer than 21 of Guy's 141 rides (nearly one in seven) ended in his pulling his horse up – indication not of a faint-hearted or less than committed pilot, but of the quality (or, rather, the lack of it) of so many of his rides. Horses are pulled up for a variety of reasons – after a bad mistake, after being forced out by a loose horse, after experiencing a physical mishap such as 'swallowing his tongue' (the phrase used to describe a temporary blockage of the horse's windpipe), etc. – but the most common is that they are simply not good enough to keep up with the others, and there's no point in (as it were) flogging a dead horse.

Or take the starting prices of Guy's rides, a reasonable indication of how their chances were perceived. Over half the horses he rode (72 of the 141) started at 20–1 or longer:

20–1: 7 rides
25–1: 10 rides
33–1: 19 rides
40–1: 3 rides
66–1: 8 rides
100–1: 8 rides
200–1: 1 ride (Prussia at Cheltenham).

Had you had £1 to win on each of the 141 rides, you would have ended the season £116.60 down.

The season which had started so full of promise for Guy Lewis had ended in frustration, but by the first Saturday of the new term his optimism had been renewed, along with his conditional jockeys' licence. A conditional's application for a licence must be backed by a trainer, and this time it was Bernard Llewellyn, a trainer with some twenty-five horses at his base in Mid Glamorgan, who became co-signatory of Guy's licence application to the Jockey Club. The licence was duly granted, and he was in business again.

Another indication of renewal was the promise of a new car, sponsored by a nearby garage.

That things were looking up was confirmed by a minor triumph – over gravity, if not over his rivals – on Guy's first ride of the 1997–8 season, at Worcester on Saturday 7 June, just a week after the end of the previous term. The eyes of most of the racing world that afternoon were focused on

Epsom Downs, where Benny The Dip and Silver Patriarch
provided their famous finish to the 1997 Derby. A jumping
meeting at Worcester could be no more than a minor
sideshow, but a ride on Chan The Man in the novice chase –
the horse's first outing since giving Guy his final winner of
the previous season at Hereford – produced a memorable
spectacle of its own.

*Chan The Man at Worcester did not have the fondest
associations for me, as it was there, in a bumper the
previous season, that he failed to negotiate the turn
into the home straight and went down the bank into
the river, where he planted himself and wouldn't budge.
This time he was well fancied – started favourite – and
I felt that if he was on song, as he had been the last
time out at Hereford, he'd win. A win in the first week
of the season would be a novelty for me!*

*It didn't work out like that, but I awarded myself the
Recovery of the Season Award – not that the season had
gone very far – after the race. Today he was at his
quirkiest. He was beginning to get worked up in the
paddock, and things went from bad to worse when we
got to the start as we were kept there a long time. Then
one of the runners charged the tapes and dislodged his
jockey, which didn't amuse Chan The Man at all: he
planted himself behind the rest of the runners, and when
I urged him to move forward to get into line he started
rearing up. He lost a few lengths when we were eventually let go but got back into the race easily enough, and
we were sat fourth over the first couple of fences.*

After his performance at Hereford I thought I could afford to be a bit more positive about his jumping – give him a kick into his fences and teach him a few things. He jumped the first two neatly, then we turned into the straight to face up to the open ditch, which he cleared well enough. But the fence after the ditch he absolutely uprooted, and skewered sideways on landing. I went straight over his head, lost my right stirrup, and was thrown out his left side, hanging on for dear life with both legs over the one side of the saddle. The law of gravity was insisting that I couldn't hang on much longer, but I was desperately trying to haul my way back into the saddle – not least because the fences in the straight at Worcester come very close together, and the next was almost upon us. Just before it I was flailing around at the same height as Chan The Man's legs, but made one almighty effort to get back aboard. It was either that or bailing out: having the horse slam me into the fence was not an option I was inclined to entertain. I somehow found the energy and the leverage to wrest myself back into the saddle but there was no time to get my right foot back into the iron before jumping the fence. We managed to get over it in one piece, then when I went to retrieve the iron I found that it had got lodged behind the saddle and was stuck there. Nothing for it but to jump the next fence without my foot in that iron, and by some miracle I managed to do so. Then, as we passed the stands with no fence to worry about for a while, I dislodged the iron and got my foot back into it – much to the appreciation of the crowd, who gave me a great cheer.

I had visions of winning and finding my way on to
A Question of Sport in the 'What Happened Next?'
slot, but there was to be no such happy ending.
Running his own race while I was busy sorting myself
out, Chan The Man had pulled his way to the front,
but down the back straight he made a horrible gurgling
noise and I had to pull him up: I think he'd swallowed
his tongue. Even then my troubles were not over: after
being pulled up Chan The Man insisted on keeping
going, over towards where the horseboxes were
parked, then showed a marked disinclination to
be taken back to the unsaddling area.

I only rode four favourites the previous season, and
now here I was on the market leader on my first ride –
and then all that happened.

After that I didn't have a ride for several days. The
trouble with summer jumping from a jockey's point of
view is that there are such long gaps between meetings,
and thus so few opportunities for rides. For days on
end I had absolutely nothing to do, and when I get
bored I start eating and drinking. During the main part
of the season you can stabilise your diet as eating
becomes simply a part of the daily routine – and not
that important a one. When there's nothing lined up,
the temptation is always there. I didn't want to get too
heavy, and without regular riding activity it's easy to
put on seven pounds before you know it. Letting your
weight rise and then having to force it down quickly
through wasting and sweating is not good for your
health generally, so you have to be careful.

One occasion when the need to watch the intake of food and alcohol could justifiably be forgotten came in June.

Throughout the season, memories of Richard Davis and his fate were never far from the thoughts of the National Hunt community. In September the Jockey Club's medical consultant Michael Turner had threatened to resign over what he saw as the lax attitude towards medical arrangements at Southwell. October saw the running of the race named in Richard's memory at Pardubice in the Czech Republic. In December there had been the inquest into his death. In May the racecourse at Hereford staged the Richard Davis Memorial Conditional Jockeys' Handicap Hurdle, after which the Richard Davis Conditional Jockeys' Memorial Award was made to Timmy Murphy as the most successful conditional jockey that season at the Three Counties courses of Cheltenham, Hereford and Worcester.

Then, on 13 June, some eleven months after Richard's death, hundreds of supporters of National Hunt racing crowded into a vast barn in the Herefordshire village of Lea, a short drive from the churchyard in Earls Croome where he had been laid to rest, for a dinner to benefit the fund which had been set up in his memory. The revellers included many of the big names of the jumping world, but to Guy Lewis went the honour of reading out a tribute to the departed jockey sent by Richard's agent and close friend Dave Roberts. The tribute closed with these words: 'Richard was one of jump racing's unsung heroes. If winners were gained by hard work and effort, then Richard would have been a National Hunt star. Unfortunately he was never given the chance others had, but never complained and always gave his best with the chances he was given. I'm sure his many friends and colleagues in racing would agree when I say that Richard will always be in our thoughts and sadly missed. However painful his absence may be, let us never forget that he gave his life for his love of National Hunt racing.'

Memories of Richard were prominent, too, the following weekend when Guy went out again to the Czech Republic, to ride at the Czech Gold Cup meeting at Pardubice – just as he, Richard, Chris Maude and Keith Dempsey had done a year before. This Czech excursion came hard on the heels of his first visit to Norway, and the life of the jet-setting jump jockey was not going smoothly.

I bet Frankie Dettori's travels are easier than this.

There were four of us on the trip to Norway: Chris Maude, Simon Burrough, Tom Dascombe and me. We flew to Oslo, but our luggage hadn't managed to make it on to the same plane and didn't turn up in Oslo until after we'd ridden, so we had to borrow all our kit from local jockeys. They were really good about it – even after Simon Burrough won the race we were riding in. After racing it was out for a night on the town in Oslo. I got back to the hotel at five in the morning, which was plenty late enough as we had to be up half an hour later to get a taxi to the airport for the flight back to London.

Then, with Dave Dent's brother Adrian, I caught my plane for the Czech Republic. We arrived in Prague and caught a taxi to the railway station for the trip out to Pardubice – but it turned out to be the wrong station.

*Eventually we found the right station, but then got on
the wrong train. It was going to Pardubice all right, but
was not the regular service taking an hour and a half: it
was a desperately slow train taking over twice that.
Worse, it was full of all sorts of dodgy-looking people,
and it was a great relief to get to Pardubice, even if by
then it was well after midnight. We took a taxi to our
hotel, arriving in time for a couple of hours at a party
hosted by the racecourse, which was already in full
swing. Eventually we got to bed.*

*The following morning I went out to the course to
ride a couple of horses, and later rode in the qualifying
race for October's Velka Pardubicka, over pretty much
the same course as the big race itself but missing out
(thank God!) the Taxis. My horse got round, but four
or five other runners that afternoon were less lucky and
were killed. That can be a cruel course for horses.*

*Just one ride that trip, which suited me fine. As soon
as I got changed I went up to catch the tail end of a
modelling session hosted by the racecourse in one of the
private bars: I was too late for the lingerie display but
got there in time for the swimwear! That evening we
went out to a restaurant just outside Pardubice, and then
to a club with the intriguing name of Gimlet, and from
there to yet another club until about six in the morning.*

*We were supposed to be taken into Prague for the
Czech Derby the following day – the same day – but
mercifully, given the state of some of our heads after
the previous evening, were forgotten about, and whiled
away the time until returning to Britain.*

*Last year's June visit with Richard was one of the
great trips of my life. This time, without him, it just
wasn't the same.*

Trips to Norway and the Czech Republic were an enjoy-
able distraction, but there was no escaping the fact that by
the summer of 1997 Guy Lewis's career was stuck. He was
only twenty-two, but riding over jumps is very much a young
man's game and it would only be a couple of years before he
would be into his sporting middle age.

By the age of thirty the jump jockey is well into the elder
statesman category – unlike his counterparts on the Flat,
where it is not uncommon for a jockey to be riding well into
his fifties: Lester Piggott first retired in 1985 at the age of
forty-nine, then in October 1990 returned to the saddle three
weeks short of his fifty-fifth birthday, and last rode in Britain
on the day he was fifty-nine; Willie Carson was fifty-three
when he had his last ride in 1996.

The key difference between riding under the respective
codes is of course that Flat jockeys fall off less, whereas for
the jump jockey there is a limit to how long your body will
take the bumps, bruises and breaks which are part of the job
description. John Francome was thirty-two when he retired
in 1985; Peter Scudamore thirty-four when he brought his
record-breaking career to a close in April 1993. At the end
of the 1996–7 season the senior jump jockey in the weighing
room was Simon McNeill, still going strong at forty-one.

Simon McNeill is himself an interesting example of a
phenomenon which may sustain the imagination of the
aspiring jump jockey: the association with one very good

horse. In McNeill's case it was the brilliant two-miler chaser Katabatic, whom he rode to win several races, including the Queen Mother Champion Chase at the Cheltenham Festival in 1991. Yet Katabatic came along too late to lift him into the top flight: in his best ever season, 1991–2, he rode thirty-one winners.

For all the journeyman's dreams, the stark fact is that most jump jockeys who reach the top flight get there very early, rather than work their way up through the ranks. Peter Scudamore, winningmost jump jockey of all, rode the first of his career total of 1,678 winners in November 1979 and was champion jockey for the first time – sharing the title with John Francome – just two and a half years later. Richard Dunwoody became first jockey to the powerful David Nicholson stable only three years after scoring his first win under Rules, and was soon riding a string of big-race winners. Most spectacularly of all in the modern era, Tony McCoy was champion jockey in his first season as a fully fledged rider, having been champion conditional (with seventy-four winners, a record for a conditional) the year before. The lesson seems to be: break fast.

But all riding careers, whether they climb steeply to the stratosphere or remain closer to street level, come to an end eventually, and like many sportsmen jump jockeys face the problem of how to structure a new life once they have retired from the sport. As a sample of alternative futures, consider the top dozen jockeys from ten years ago, the kings of the 1986–7 season. Several are still riding, but the current careers of those who have retired from the saddle provide a reasonable indication of what a jump jockey might do. Peter

Scudamore is a journalist and BBC racing pundit, as well as assisting Nigel Twiston-Davies in his training operation in Gloucestershire. Steve Smith Eccles also works in the media. Richard Rowe and Chris Grant are trainers, Simon Sherwood assistant trainer to his brother Oliver. Sam Morshead is Clerk of the Course at two Scottish tracks. Phil Tuck is a stewards' secretary.

Most jockeys stay in racing in some role or other. Ron Barry and Richard Linley are course inspectors; Gerry Scott (who won the Grand National on Merryman II in 1960) is a starter; John Buckingham, as we have seen, is a valet. Some have made their mark beyond the immediate confines of the sport: Dick Francis, phenomenally successful crime writer, or Philip Blacker, sculptor.

For all his occasional bouts of gloom, Guy Lewis considers thoughts of stopping absurdly premature, but it's as well to be prepared.

A lot of jockeys have nothing when they retire, but you have to think about the future, and over the last year I've been making use of the Jockeys' Employment and Training Scheme (JETS) to acquire computer skills. With two 'A' levels already under my belt, I shouldn't be totally unqualified to take on something else when I stop riding, though at the moment I have no serious idea what that might be.

Dai Tegg said to me not long ago: However badly you're going, don't think of packing up. He's right. Whatever the risks, and however great the exasperations and disappointments, the life is so good it's worth all the downside. The racing itself gives me a real buzz, there's a great social life – jump jockeys attract lots of groupies as we're so brave and handsome! – and I earn enough to afford the occasional decent night out.

It's a young person's life – a bit like being at university – and it won't last long. The risks are always there, but you can get run over by a car any day of the week. Why not enjoy yourself?

8

A Day at the Races

'I'd better go and get my bollocking'

FRIDAY, 18 JULY 1997.

For racegoers arriving early for today's jumping meeting at Southwell, the presence of the two ambulances waiting near the weighing room has a special significance. And the name of the first race on the afternoon's card rings a bell. The Fisherton Novices' Handicap Chase. This is the very programme, that was the race, which cost Richard Davis his life a year ago.

Nowhere is the anniversary more keenly felt than in the weighing room, where from an hour before the first race the jockeys riding that day – only twenty-three of them, with just thirty-eight runners in the six races – start to arrive. Each of them, whether it be Tony McCoy or a seven-pound claiming amateur, shows his riding licence and medical book to the Declarations Clerk, a homely lady who sits at a table by the door and checks the jockeys in.

Inside the changing room itself the atmosphere is subdued.

Most of the riders are conscious of the significance of the day, but in any case low-key days at the races do not come much lower-key than this. With little to get excited about, small groups of jockeys huddle on the benches, half dressed in breeches, shirts and body protectors, smoking and chatting.

Of the seven jockeys with rides in the Fisherton Novices' Handicap Chase today, two also took part in the race last year. One of these, Richard Guest, is featured in an article in this morning's *Racing Post*, drawing attention to the anniversary: 'It will give me great pleasure if I can win the race this time. I shall be trying my hardest not just for myself but for Richard as well. I am sure it will be the same for all the jockeys in the race.'

This is a quiet day's racing – a *very* quiet day – not only for the jockeys but for the others who keep the show on the road. Some of them, indeed, lament the fact that the show is still on the road at all, rather than decently put away under wraps for a couple of months as it used to be, allowing the jockeys a brief relaxation of the iron dietary discipline to which they subject themselves for the rest of the year. Even so, as the intensity of the spring action is replaced by the desultory succession of summer meetings, some of them do take a bit of a breather – as senior valet John Buckingham, no fan of summer jumping, is well placed to notice ('Look at all those fat jockeys!'); for him, as for so many others, Southwell on a warm July afternoon is a 'piddling' fixture.

Maybe, but a crowd several hundred strong is enjoying ambling around in the sunshine, studying the horses in the pre-parade ring with none of the crush of a busier meeting, finding it easy to get a good view of the action and ready access to the bar. The major business of Southwell these days is to stage all-weather Flat racing on the track which runs outside the turf steeplechase and hurdle course. (At Southwell the hurdles are not, as at most courses, like sheep hurdles, but more like junior steeplechase fences.) Admittedly the course has a total lack of the atmosphere and rural charm of the best gaffs – Kelso, say, or Cartmel or Ludlow or Hexham – but there is still a very local feel to the racegoing crowd here, and the course is making visible efforts to provide a congenial setting, with plenty of shrubs and trees around the paddock area.

Back in the changing room, Guy Lewis emerges from the sauna, a towel round his body and not a visible spare ounce on his frame. Like his friend a year ago, he has come to Southwell for just one ride. His partner in the second race is our old friend Chan The Man, pulled up in his last two races but before that, at Hereford, the slightly unexpected provider of Guy's fifth and final winner of last season. Chan The Man's form since that win has been – on paper, if not in the eyes of his jockey – less than inspiring, and it is no surprise to find him at the foot of the handicap, down to carry ten stone. Take off the three-pound allowance, and for Guy it's the old story of getting his body weight down to nine eight and riding with a postage-stamp-sized saddle. In addition, Chan The Man's owners have been wondering whether the horse's wayward tendencies might not be due to pain in his back, and have suggested that today he race with a jelly-pad (a pad filled with a synthetic gel) under his saddle to relieve the pressure. This jelly-pad might make the horse more comfortable, but it weighs perhaps three pounds – three more pounds that Guy has to try to sweat off in the sauna.

By the time the first race is run, Guy has dressed in his colours and checked his weight on the trying scales. The 1997 renewal of the Fisherton Novices' Handicap Chase seems to have attracted a field of about as woeful a standard as that of 1996, and the jockeys watching the race on the television set in the changing room see a typical bottom-drawer novice chase. The jumping of most of the seven runners is haphazard, and only three of them complete the course: Richard Guest's mount Fenwick's Brother repays his jockey's hopes by falling at the third last, two pull up and another unseats his rider.

The riders come back, the first three weigh in, and within a few minutes the eight who are riding in the Appleyard & Trew Handicap Chase, over two miles and worth £4,667 to the winner, file out of the changing room and present themselves at the scales for the moment of truth.

Guy takes his seat. The Clerk of the Scales checks that he is wearing the correct declared colours for Chan The Man – light blue, white star, halved sleeves, white star on cap – then addresses himself to the tricky matter of Guy's weight. The needle on the huge circular face of the scales has swung over the ten stone mark, seemed to kiss ten two and then shuddered back to ten one. 'We'll say ten stone,' declares the Clerk of the Scales – making allowance for the one pound of body protector – and ten stone is the weight which duly goes into the Clerk's book. Since his allowance should have brought Chan The Man's burden down to nine eleven, Guy has put up three pounds overweight.

The saddle is passed by Guy to Dai Burchell, son of Chan The Man's trainer. Later in the afternoon Dai junior is due to ride a mare named Henrietta Boo Boo for his father in the selling hurdle, but first he has to assist in the saddling of Chan The Man, and having taken the saddle from the jockey he makes his way to the pre-parade ring, where the runners for the race are being quietly led round.

And here is Chan The Man himself. If looks counted for much in racing, this horse would not be the outsider in a novice chase at Southwell: a son of the American stallion Krisinsky (and thus a grandson of the great Nijinsky) and a half-brother to Channel Pastime, Chan The Man is a handsome six-year-old bay gelding, with a fine physique and a noble head. It's what's inside that head that's the problem, though: what kink is there in Chan The Man's cerebral region which has caused him to run into the river with Guy at Worcester or to lug him into the horsebox park at the same course? We can't know; but consider him walking round now, remember how he won at Hereford only a few weeks ago, and his current price of 33–1 with the Southwell bookmakers does not seem so unappealing.

First, though, he needs to be got ready. As Chan The Man is led into the stall to be saddled, Dai Burchell senior comes up with a bucket of water and a sponge. On seeing the size of Guy's tiny saddle he swears – hadn't they asked him to ride on a larger saddle if he could manage it? – but it's too late to do anything now, and with Dai junior one side of the horse, Dai senior the other and Chan The Man's stable lad at his head, the tack is put on: first the jelly-bag, then the number cloth, then the saddle itself, held in place by the girth, tightened by buckles under the saddle flaps, and a surcingle, a strap which goes right round the horse's belly and over the saddle. When the tack is in place Dai senior fills the sponge with water and sloshes it into the horse's mouth – in the process depositing half of it into the face of the stable lad standing the other side.

As the horse is led off towards the parade ring, Ashley Bealby, Clerk of the Course at Southwell, comes up to Dai: will his horse be taking the practice jump?

One of the recommendations of the Jockey Club inquiry into the Richard Davis tragedy was that courses might consider installing a practice jump for horses to take on their way to the start if their trainers and jockeys so wished. Although there was some resistance to the idea, it was realised that in certain cases it might help a jockey to pop an unfamiliar horse over a small fence before the race (Richard had never jumped an obstacle on Mr Sox), and Southwell was the first course to provide this facility, as an experiment. And so it is that halfway up the Southwell straight on this July Friday, facing in (as it were) the wrong direction, sits a narrow little practice fence.

Soon after reaching the parade ring Dai Burchell senior is joined by Guy, who receives simple riding instructions – 'try not to pull him around' – and a direction to pop Chan The Man over the practice jump.

'Riders for the second race please mount!' – and Guy is legged up into the saddle.

Out on the course, Chan The Man is shown the practice jump, then turns, canters back half a furlong and, accompanied by Sigma Run, nips over it neatly enough, turns back towards the stands and canters round to the start at the far side of the track.

In the early stages of the race Chan The Man's jumping is uneven: some fences he measures well and jumps fluently; at others he gets in too close. For about a mile he is still in touch with the leaders, but as they approach the end of the back straight he is clearly getting detached from the business end of the race. Guy's arm goes up in the air and *thwack!* delivers a less than hopeful reminder to his horse that now is the time to dig deep. No response. *Thwack!* again, but halfway round the final bend the leaders are already beyond recall, and there is nothing for it but to let Chan The Man come back in his own time.

There are four fences left to be jumped in the straight. Chan The Man pops over the fourth last, pops over the third last – then, at the second last, fails to get high enough, and though he manages to land on the other side in an untidy heap, Guy has no chance of staying on. It looks like a fall, but the form book will classify it as 'unseated rider'.

Chan The Man, none the worse for his escapade, lollops off towards the finishing line, where he is retrieved and taken back to the saddling area to be washed down. Meanwhile Guy and fellow jockey Michael Brennan, whose mount Sigma Run had unseated him at the second last, colliding with the eventual winner Jazzy Refrain, trudge back along the course.

Guy is not happy. 'Great, isn't it? I've hardly eaten for two days, I've wasted like mad to do the weight, and that's what happens. That horse is knackered. They won't be pleased with me. Oh well – I'd better go and get my bollocking . . .'

In the bar later with fellow jockeys the gossip, as so often, is of rides, of trainers, of who will work for whom this season. There is also talk about the conditions under which the aspiring jockey has to work in order to gain access to that precious supply of rides.

A young lady amateur rider, with several winners to her name, is thinking about ways of moving on from her present position. 'I'm earning £130 per week and I don't live in, so I have to find my own accommodation out of that. I work from six-thirty in the morning until one in the afternoon, then three-thirty in the afternoon until six, and I get one day off every two weeks. They class you as unskilled labour – but they should try getting some guy in off the street and ask him to gallop a two-year-old who's only just been broken, or school a daft novice over three fences.' Her left shoulder is strapped up following a fall on the gallops: 'The boss didn't want to school it.'

Perhaps influenced by a somewhat dispirited mood, the talk moves to when jump jockeys might retire, and what they might do when their riding days are over. The bar furnishes a couple of examples: ex-riders Micky Hammond and Graham McCourt, now both trainers; Tom Morgan, who as rider of Yahoo against Desert Orchid in the 1989 Cheltenham Gold Cup so nearly spoiled the greatest explosion of Dessiemania, but was then forced to retire from the saddle because of weight problems, and is now assistant to Graham McCourt.

Guy recalls that he's come all the way to the Nottinghamshire course, just as Richard had a year ago, for just one ride; an additional coincidence is that, as with Richard last year, he is due to go to a wedding the following day. And he points out, with regard to the practice fence, that in his race the two jockeys who were unseated were 'the only idiots who took the schooling fence'.

While Guy has been musing in the bar, the fifth race has been run, in which the other Dai Burchell runner of the day, Henrietta Boo Boo, was ridden by Dai junior. What happened? The mare refused to line up with the other runners and was withdrawn at the start. What a waste of a journey! 'You could have ridden that one,' sighs young Dai to Guy back in the weighing room.

Time to go home. In the car park a man shouts out: 'What size shirt are you?!' He is selling (or failing to sell) shirts out of the boot of his car, claiming that he has just had a big winner and the bookmaker has paid him in shirts rather than cash. When his sales pitch – 'Fiver a shirt, lads!' – is greeted with genial scepticism, he points out that he also has a nifty line in watches. 'Come on, now, these are high-quality watches. I'm a friend of Michael Tabor!'

Every racecourse has its characters. Even Southwell.

Guy slings his riding bag into the back of the blue Mondeo, gets in, and heads for the endless straight road which leads from the racecourse back towards civilization. The rear bumper proclaiming the occupant as GUY LEWIS – NATIONAL HUNT CONDITIONAL JOCKEY zooms away into the distance.

Nice day at the office, dear?

9

The Best Job in the World

'There's just nothing like it'

S O WHY DO THEY DO IT?
We've heard about the horses so badly trained that they haven't a clue how to jump; about the exasperating trainers who offer you rides one day and cold-shoulder you the next; about the paltry remuneration; about the long, long hours in the car, the sauna and the hot bath; about the senior jockeys who bawl you out when your wretched partner gets in their way; about how, just when you have a hard-earned victory in your grasp, along comes Richard Dunwoody in full growl to pip you at the post; about changes in the weather that can leave you unemployed for weeks on end; about the horse who treads on your eye as he gets up having deposited you on the ground, adding injury to insult.

We've heard about the extraordinarily high level of risk and the extraordinarily low level of reward. We've even heard about death in action.

So why do they do it?

Ask a silly question – and get Guy Lewis to answer it.

When everything goes right, there's nothing to compare with riding over fences, no experience so exhilarating. It's simply the best job in the world.

No one wants to get hurt, but the risks of race riding are a part of what makes the life so exciting, gives it such a buzz.

When that buzz diminishes, that's the time to think about quitting. Being a jump jockey is for young men, and few get very far into their thirties before they find they don't bounce quite so nimbly, don't get back from injury quite so quickly, find themselves thinking that every fall is one too many.

And yet when you're riding a horse that jumps well, doesn't put a foot wrong in a race and pings every fence, there's just nothing like it. Coming to the second last full of running and taking it up going to the last to win by twenty lengths – that's a pretty good feeling. But winning on the bridle can be a little bit too easy, and for me the greatest buzz comes when you've got to get stuck in a little to get a result, when you make a bit of a race of it – coming to the third last flat out and upsides, and you both throw your horses over the last three fences before you go on to win.

I got exactly that buzz when riding What's In Orbit in a chase at Wincanton in April 1995. Trained by Paul Nicholls, What's In Orbit was a really good two-mile chaser, and like many jockeys I like nothing more than a two-mile chase. You're going a brisk gallop all the way, and it's your jumping that keeps your momentum going. A two-mile chase is the chasing equivalent of a sprint, and there's very little time to recover if you get the jumping wrong.

What's In Orbit had enormous scope: going into a fence, you could pick him up from anywhere. I won on him a couple of times, but this Wincanton race left me on a high that lasted for days afterwards.

There were only three runners, but one of these was a very good chaser trained by Nicky Henderson, Billy Bathgate. I made most of the running on What's In Orbit and he stood off at every fence – ping!, ping!, ping! Turning into the home straight I gave him a slight breather, which allowed Billy Bathgate to get upsides, then set him alight for the last three fences. Billy Bathgate was sticking to me, but I thought I'd take him on over those final fences.

At the third last I went quite long and kept Billy Bathgate at bay; at the second last I went long again and my fellow picked up brilliantly, but we still hadn't shaken off the other horse. So I rode to the last fence hell for leather and threw What's in Orbit at it as if it were a hurdle, got a couple of lengths and made enough ground to win going away.

Brilliant!

If I ever need to remind myself why I'm in this game, I just think of that race. It wasn't a Grand National or a Gold Cup, it didn't make me rich and famous, but the feeling it gave me, that sensation of complete co-ordination with my horse, of being able to control and channel *his strength and athleticism, meeting every fence right and beating off his rivals, was just fantastic.*

And you don't have to win to get that buzz. My ride around Aintree on Channel Pastime in the John Hughes Trophy may not have landed me in the winner's enclosure, or brought me that extra credit entry on my Weatherbys account, but what a great experience! Time after time I've rewound the video to marvel at the way he attacked the Canal Turn, and every time the buzz comes back.

That's *why I do it.*

The life of the journeyman jump jockey may be about trainers and owners and stewards and clerks of the scales and punters and – most of all – horses. But beyond those day-to-day relationships it is about spirit.

It took a while for Richard Davis's parents to bring themselves to clear their son's house of his belongings, but when they did so, his mother found attached to a pinboard a small card bearing a picture of a bear struggling to climb up a snow-capped mountain. The verse on the card promulgated a simple message:

When things go wrong as they sometimes will,
When the road you're trudging seems all uphill,
When the funds are low and the debts are high,
And you want to smile but you have to sigh,
When care is pressing you down a bit,
Rest, if you must, but don't you quit . . .

Ann Davis did not know where Richard had got this card, but for her it seemed to epitomise his attitude to his work. Keep going. Aspiration is all.

To win just once –
That would be enough.

Postscript

To Win Just Twice

THE 1997–8 SEASON WHICH HAD BEGUN FOR GUY with that acrobatic recovery on Chan The Man at Worcester on Derby Day 1997 ended on Time Can Tell in the exotically named Caradon Plumbing Solutions Novices' Hurdle at Uttoxeter at the end of May 1998, nearly a year later. Like eighty-six of his eighty-eight rides in Britain that term, Time Can Tell failed to win.

It was not until Saturday 6 December 1997 – a day short of six months since Guy's first ride of the season – that he rode a winner. The aficionados had gone to Sandown Park for the clash of Ask Tom, Viking Flagship and Klairon Davis in the Tingle Creek Chase. The Pury End Conditional Jockeys Handicap Hurdle at Towcester was humbler fare, and the blinkered Ainsi Soit Il, a six-year-old gelding trained by Graham McCourt, hardly in the Viking Flagship class: it took a deal of pushing and shoving up that endless Towcester hill to keep his nose in front, but the horse responded gamely and held on.

On Monday 8 December, the very next racing day, the

Weatherbys computer was again whirring into action to work out the winning percentage to be credited to the account of Guy Lewis: Galloping Guns had scored a half-length victory in a conditional jockeys' hurdle at Ludlow. Guy was on a roll.

Winners breed rides. After both those races I was interviewed on the Racing Channel, which must have brought me back into the minds of a few trainers who had forgotten all about me, and by the end of December I'd had twenty rides that month. Twenty every month would have been very healthy, but it didn't last.

It certainly didn't. January brought six rides, February seven. Guy was getting forgotten again, and the hope that more winners would raise his profile proved a forlorn one. There were no more. By the official end of the season on 30 May 1998, Guy's brace of winners left him 251 behind the record-breaking champion jockey Tony McCoy. Guy had had 88 rides, McCoy 831.

It had been a terrible season, and even its most abiding memory was one of undignified failure.

In October I was the only English jockey to take part in the Velka Pardubicka, but I soon wished I hadn't! Baddellios was a chance ride, and I'd never sat on him until I got the leg up in the paddock. It didn't take me long to work out that this horse had a brain problem: in fact he was a complete nutcase. When the lad leading him let him go on the way to the start, he pissed off in the wrong direction, and the only way I could get him down was by shoving him up the arse of the horse in front. I knew I'd have problems holding him in the race, but the last thing I wanted was to hit the front early on: although I'd walked the course enough times, I'd only reached the fourth fence – the Taxis – last year, and I couldn't be guaranteed to know my way round on a bonkers tearaway. So I thought I'd try to keep him covered up towards the rear. Some hope! By the time we reached the first he was mid-division, by the second he was fourth or fifth, by the water jump he was in contention for the lead, and on the run towards the Taxis he was in front and completely out of control. He launched himself at the fence, cleared it, and as he descended on to the lip of the ditch, his head came up and I was shot out of the saddle. For a moment I was hanging on for dear life – then I let go, slid off and landed on my backside. Not a very elegant end, but better, in the circumstances, than staying on and trying to negotiate him over the fearsome bank which came next. It was a relief to be in one piece.

Baddellios was one of twelve overseas rides in Guy's season which brought his total to a round 100.

Financially it was a disastrous time – the first season in which I've made a loss – and it got depressing as the supply of rides became a trickle, but there are plenty of other jockeys like me, and plenty of good horses to ride in the new season.

If I can get on them . . .

Index